You're NOT Disordered

The Ultimate Wellbeing Guide

for Bloggers

As with a lot of media content related to mental health, this Guide may contain upsetting language or details of difficult experiences. If you are struggling with these aspects of the Guide, please seek appropriate help and support.

Any events in this Guide have been relayed to the best of the Author's ability.

You're NOT Disordered

And you said that I was done,

Well you were wrong,

And now,

The best is yet to come

Ke$ha - Praying

A Note From Award-Winning Blogger, Aimee Wilson...

I created my blog; I'm NOT Disordered in January 2013, at a time when there were only three well-known mental health blogs (none of which were written by a current psychiatric hospital inpatient as I was then). Having no one to really look to as some sort of head's up to kind of lead the way and provide me with some straightforward influence and inspiration has meant that I definitely feel I've learnt a lot of things in blogging the hard way.

This opinion has led me to be very passionate and eager to spread the knowledge I have gained from my blogging experience that now spans over ten years, and it is this, which has motivated me to create You're Not Disordered.

I feel that the most important lessons I've learnt from the blogging industry, aren't about how to write a product review or how to add different technical features to your blog. So, the essential lessons I want to publicise are about coping and managing your mental health and general wellbeing amongst all the tasks, challenges, and opportunities that arise from blogging.

I think that the reason for the importance of this advice I have, is largely linked to the fact that I've found that when I'm safe and healthy in myself, this usually influences the content I produce. So, utilising coping skills and developing resources to look to for help and support throughout your blogging journey, can therefore then lend themselves to actually also improving the quality, success, and popularity of your blog.

So, I really hope that this Guide helps you and your blog to make your own mark on the digital world!

Foreword by Martin Baker

I first met Aimee Wilson in February 2016 when I volunteered with the mental health campaign Time to Change. Aimee was running the social media for the event. Our friendship is rooted in our mutual interest in mental health and passion for blogging. I'm delighted to have this opportunity to contribute a few words on her wellbeing guide for bloggers.

In her previous book, *Everything Disordered: A Practical Guide to Blogging*, Aimee shared tips and guidance on a range of topics, such as whether blogging is right for you, writing and publishing posts, collaborating with individuals and organisations, event blogging, and working with the press and media. Always honest about the challenges associated with sharing online, Aimee showed how social media in general, and blogging in particular, can nevertheless be immensely positive and beneficial.

Aimee explores this further in her new book, *You're NOT Disordered: The Ultimate Wellbeing Guide for Bloggers*. No matter what you write about, growing and maintaining a successful blog involves many different skills, disciplines, and practices. Keeping on top of things can demand a lot of time, energy, and focus. As I know myself, it's easy to feel discouraged, pressured, and even overwhelmed at times.

Aimee is no stranger to these challenges, having run a highly successful blog for more than ten years. Using examples from her own experience, she helps the reader think about the challenges they may face and develop healthy coping strategies. The book focuses on blogging, but these skills are useful in any areas of our lives where we feel stressed, anxious, or uncertain.

The book addresses difficult scenarios such as handling negative feedback, competition, jealousy, and disappointment. It may be less obvious, but positive situations, opportunities, and successes can also be challenging, and Aimee covers these too.

One of our strengths as friends is that we offer each other suggestions and advice when asked but feel able to adapt or ignore that advice if it doesn't work for us. The wisdom of this approach is made clear early in the book, with sections on the unspoken rules of advice in blogging, and how to handle things if advice doesn't work out for you.

Overall, Aimee shows how paying attention to our mental health and wellbeing not only helps us personally, but also contributes to producing higher quality content for our followers. Whether you're a seasoned blogger with years of writing behind you, just starting out on your blogging journey, or wondering if blogging is for you, this guide will help you on your way. I'll certainly keep my copy close to hand!

Martin Baker

Martin Baker, co-author with Fran Houston of *High Tide, Low Tide: The Caring Friend's Guide to Bipolar Disorder* and *No One Is Too Far Away: Notes from a Transatlantic Friendship*, is a mental health author and blogger living in North-East England. Martin blogs about mental health and supportive friendships at: www.gumonmyshoe.com

"Never give advice unless you have walked the walk, because anybody can talk the talk"

Valencia Mackie

The Importance of Advice During The Early Days

Someone from my local mental health NHS Trust (Cumbria, Northumberland, Tyne and Wear NHS Foundation Trust, who are known better, and more simply, as CNTW) once contacted me to tell me that one of their service users was keen to start blogging. They were asking whether I'd be willing to be some sort of mentor for this person and give her a little bit of advice and coaching to help her into the blogging world.

Now, I'm fully aware that I hold an attitude that is quite rare amongst bloggers in that I love the idea of encouraging others to join the industry and I enjoy offering whatever tips that I can to help improve their experience of blogging. For a lot of bloggers, this is seen as a little bit stupid and self-sabotaging. As though, any other blog should be viewed as competition and nothing more. I, however, like to see other bloggers (especially new ones) as inspirational and influential.

So, after agreeing to take on the mentor role with the CNTW service user, I made contact with the girl and almost started to tell her about the various platforms she could use to host her blog, when I realised I'd missed the first, most crucial part of starting to blog. Upon realising this, before continuing, I asked her to read a few of my three-part series of blog posts that were titled; 'Everything You Need To Know Before You Start Blogging.' I explained to her that this was such an important first step because I wouldn't want anyone to get into this industry with as little expectation and knowledge as I had when I created I'm NOT Disordered.

Of course, when I started blogging, with there being so few other mental health blogs, there was no one to really turn to as a means of developing a real idol or resource to go to for ideas, guidance, advice, trends… It was as though I was just thrown in at the deep end or had been stood on my feet before I'd even learnt how to crawl!

Fortunately, for two reasons, I was able to cope with this:

1. I was surrounded by the staff and other inpatients in the psychiatric hospital which meant I always had support and someone to talk to
2. The lack of other mental health blogs meant there was no real stress or pressure that I wasn't figuring things out quick enough to keep up with the industry

The fact I had these helpful elements to my life and my mental health, I'm still very aware that these definifely aren't something a lot of prospective bloggers will have. So, my motivation to encourage someone to think about the consequences and difficulties they might experience should they begin blogging, is really based on that – the fact that not everyone will have the tools and resources to be capable of coping.

In addition to the inability to safely manage any thoughts and feelings around challenigng experiences in blogging, now that the blogging world is so much bigger and so much more competitive, thinking that you'll just learn as you go isn't always the best or most practical path to take when you're deciding to blog. It could very well lead you to the notion that you're falling behind trends and your blog is becoming irrelevant and outdated which can very easily affect the size of your audience and your blog's general standing and reputation in the industry.

Recognising that failing to think ahead and prepare yourself for anything challenging in the blogging world can affect both your wellbeing and the impact your blog has, definitley proves the importance of doing these things.

Coping If The Advice Fails

In this day and age, being transparent, honest, and open in the digital sphere is an incredibly favoured approach that so many readers and followers demand from the content created by bloggers, YouTubers, and other online influencers. I think that some readers have a sense of entitlement (that definitely isn't misplaced) where they really believe that if they're going to follow a person or an organisation and invest in any products they advertise, then they deserve to know the truth behind the posts regarding them. They like to be aware of how the online influencer themselves is benefiting from the content and often use this as a means of determining just how appealing the advertorial is.

So, with that in mind, I thought it would be a good idea to include a little piece about coping if you take advice and feel that it fails before I tell you all the blogging advice that I would give.

Now, I honestly think that it's fair to say that the notion of 'failure' can actually be a common thought or feeling to frequently battle in your blogging journey. Especially in the early days because that's the period of time where you're really just testing the waters a lot whilst trying to find your footing in the industry. That stage in your blogging career is so essential in helping you to figure out what works for you and your blog, and what doesn't work. The only way to do this, is by trying; and it stands to reason that not every single attempt is going to be a complete success or a total hit.

I think that similarly to how accepting that you need help is so important in the process of improving something; recognising the realistic possible result or consequence of something can really drive how you think and feel. If you're aware that your decision might be unsuccessful, you might have a much more effective experience when you decide to try out a piece of advice. It'll make the entire process a whole lot less difficult for your mental health too if you have some kind of notion in being prepared and expectant.

Coping with something though – especially when it's something that could either crush your spirit or teach you an important lesson – means that sometimes failure and expecting it, might be the way it is with grief. In that you often hear people say that it's easier when you know a person is going to die because it's not really a surprise that will catch you off-guard. This really isn't always the case. In fact, it can be completely to the contrary and expecting something terrible, can flaw your mood to the point where you either change your mind completely or push through it and feel so completely stupid for persisting.

Aside from considering there'll be bad consequences in taking advice can often help you to cope when that does happen; is useful, there are – thankfully – additional, more mental and emotional tools that can be helpful too...

Firstly, it's incredibly important to have an understanding of the difference between blame and responsibility, and be able to recognise which of these is at play in your situation. I very much doubt I'm the only person in the world, but believe when I say that if you want to talk to someone who's a huge user of self-blame, look no further than me! Throughout the worst years of my mental health, I was almost constantly blaming myself for absolutely anything and everything that 'went wrong.'

That – almost, habit – became so debilitating by having a huge influence on my unsafe thoughts and feelings. Thinking that things were solely my fault, left me feeling worthless and hopeless – two feelings that are very rarely useful or pleasant for your mental health. It meant that when professionals began lecturing me about not taking responsibility for my actions, I was confused; I thought that doing that was the problem. But there was a difference and all of the blame I bestowed upon myself actually wasn't even correct. The psychiatric professionals explained that the two areas (the abuse I experienced when I was younger and my self-harm and suicide attempts) weren't at all my fault. I had been a 'victim' of the abuse and my self-harm etc was due to me being poorly.

The areas I should be responsible for though, were the actions and reactions that I had a real choice about – even when it sometimes felt as though I didn't. I learnt that rather than doing something and saying "I only did this because of what you did," you should instead recognise why the behaviours of someone else, or why the details of a situation you're in, have led you to feeling this way and doing whatever it is you do to cope with these thoughts and feelings.

This discussion of responsibility around advice 'failing' is relevant to ensuring that you recognise whether the advice you've tried to implement hasn't worked because of something you have done with it. For example, if you've made a tweak to it, or thought it needed a new spin and some editing so that it worked in continuity with your blog specifically. It could be the other way around too – perhaps you took the advice very literally and it might have been better suited for you and your blog if you'd utilised it with a slightly different method or approach.

In establishing your level (even if it's none) of responsibility in the failure of any advice and having some sort of warning about the possibility of it anyway, another skill for coping with the failure of advice, can be using the experience to help others in whatever way is appropriate/relevant – whether it's about writing an entire blog post or simply posting a tweet. The notion that a hardship you've experienced can be completely turned on itself and made into something useful for others, can be incredibly therapeutic.

You're NOT Disordered

This thought process is very obviously something which I do myself for many different experiences I've had (even those which I wouldn't have labelled as a 'failure'!). My use of this coping skill, massively stems from all that I went through when I finally reported the abuse I had experienced to the Police. Of course it was an incredibly difficult, challenging, and almost debilitating experience to have to – effectively – relive the entire trauma over and over again (and in a huge amount of detail) for the different methods of recording a statement and being interviewed etc.

A great reason for the struggle during this part of my life was that, whilst it was such a horrendous experience for me to go through, I knew that it was the 'right' thing to do. Aside from eventually believing the psychiatric professionals who encouraged the mindset that talking about it would be a massive step forward on the road to mental health recovery, I also recognised what my report would mean for others (and, to be honest, that was the largest motivation for me). I knew that my allegation alone – even if he wasn't prosecuted – would lead to people being more wary and cautious of having any kind of relationship with the man who abused me. This filled me with the hope that I had the power and potential to make it a lot more difficult for him to go on to inflict the same abuse on someone else.

The gravity of the benefits I have received from the knowledge that me talking about my trauma could be helpful for others, has been astronomical! I think it has been one of the greatest influences on my recovery, and so; I would highly recommend that people use their hardships as a means to – in whatever way possible – help others to avoid going through those same experiences.

This makes the notion lend itself really well to viewing these 'failures' in a more productive light; and seeing them as learning curves instead. As opportunities which you can – and should – grasp eagerly with both hands and passionately use and adapt to yours and your blog's advantage in whatever way this means for you both. For example, if you followed the advice to start creating and including images in your blog posts, but received negative comments from your readers who said they'd rather you just stick with focusing on the text because the imagery was distracting. So, you could take that lesson that your readers don't care for graphics, and use it as motivation to perhaps channel more creativity into your writing or – if you're determined for it to be visual – your blog's design and appearance.

Other Bloggers as a Source of Advice, Inspiration, & Influence

A hugely important aspect of advice – because it isn't all about what the advice actually is – is where/who it comes from. Who the actual source of your advice is, can say so much about a number of elements that are essential to take into consideration before deciding whether or not to act on what is being advised, suggested, or recommended:

1. How trustworthy and genuine the source is
2. The chance of the source having any ulterior motives
3. Whether there are any biases involved
4. How fundamentally practical/realistic their advice is
5. Whether their advice needs to be tweaked to suit you

For a few years, in the beginning of my own blogging career, I followed this one Influencer in particular who was going from strength to strength in terms of the quality of the content she was creating and the collaborations and opportunities she was landing. It was incredible to watch her go from filming YouTube videos and vlogs when she was living in her parents home and shopping in Primark, to now owning a home that is said to be worth over £1,000,000!

After a little while of being incredibly successful and her blog, social media accounts, and YouTube channel having a number of followers in the millions, she seemed to take a step back from the industry. It led me to the thought that she was resting on her laurels and now expected opportunities to automatically be handed to her on a silver platter. Granted, she had worked hard to get to that point, but to do that and then just sit back? Well, it wasn't a work ethic that I would like to think that I, myself, adheres to.

The fact that she does the opposite of the other influencer in sitting back after a number of achievements, is one reason why I now find the most inspiration in my role model of the blogging industry; Victoria Magrath of InTheFrow. Even now, despite the fact that she appears to be able to live off the income her online work is rewarding her with, she continues to work so hard. When she has an achievement or reaches a certain amount of followers etc., she doesn't stop working; she just goes on to aim for bigger and better!

I'd like to think that this is a way of working/blogging that I use too and because of that, I have some insight into one of the key difficulties with this method. There's a danger of it leading to you experiencing an overwhelming pressure with the concern that nothing is ever good enough. That no matter how many goals and aims you achieve, you will never feel content and satisfied with your content or even your entire blog in general! Which can end up leaving you with a pressure to work harder and harder and to devote more and more time to creating your content in an almost obsessive and desperate way rather than out of enjoyment and passion.

Aside from Victoria's work ethic, I've also found her actual content inspirational too. Some have actually voiced this as being strange... I actually only really follow one mental health blog; the others I like to keep up with and enjoy reading, are those that are centred around fashion and beauty.

The first of two key reasons why I do this, is purely that I have a genuine interest in that industry. When I was younger – at one point – I actually wanted to be a Fashion Designer and I even opted to study the Textiles module of the Art and Design course at School. After some debilitating criticism that wasn't at all constructive from my Teacher, I lost all passion for the industry and turned to the idea of being a Lawyer!

When I was in the specialist psychiatric hospital for two and a half years though, my artistic side came back to the surface as I progressed through my mental health recovery. In having Dialectical Behaviour Therapy (DBT), I received a ton of encouragement to utilise my stabilisation and to begin taking steps towards what I'd like my life to look like after my discharge from the hospital. So, not only did I resume doing my fashion drawings, but I also began looking into a career in the industry that I could aspire to achieve; Visual Merchandising.

This idea of that being a dream job stayed with me for a year or so until I created I'm NOT Disordered in 2013 and had an almost immediate notion that I had found a purpose in life. A purpose besides the conviction I'd held for years that I was destined to commit suicide as a means of highlighting the failures of psychiatric services. It honestly felt as though I now knew why I had been put on this earth. I knew why I'd gone through all that I had. It was all worth something.

Starting to blog in 2013 though, there was only really three well-known mental health blogs and none of them were written by a psychiatric hospital inpatient. So I struggled to decide who I could turn to for advice, ideas, and inspiration that would influence I'm NOT Disordered in whatever way possible. It was a bit of a lonely feeling to be honest, but it also meant that I had to use my creativity to think up ways for finding motivation and establishing some sort of role model or inspiration.

So, when I discovered InTheFrow, I was sort of in my element reading the blog because not only did Victoria mostly produce some incredibly interesting and passionate content on fashion and beauty, but she also produced some 'lifestyle' posts. To be honest – going back to why I consider Victoria to be inspirational for myself – I found both themes to be just as influential as each other in terms of providing ideas etc. for my own content.

In reading her fashion and beauty blog posts, I've found the concept of '5 Top...' or '10 Secrets to...' Sort of like advice posts... Ones with short and snappy, attractive titles. Initially, in the first two or three years of my blogging career, I was incredibly reluctant to do any sort of advice, guidance, or recommendation blog posts. I was pretty much 100% certain that if I did, they would be immediately knocked back and I'd be labelled as arrogant and patronising, and I obviously didn't want anyone to think those things of me. Nor did I want them to become disinterested in my blog and the content I created out of the belief that I was exhibiting these behaviours and having this attitude.

So, it wasn't until recent years – especially since reaching over one million readers – that I felt a touch of new confidence. I know full well that not every single reader has liked I'm NOT Disordered, but to have attracted over one million; sort of gives the hint that I must be doing something right! The new confidence this left me with, meant I was feeling more capable and entitled to share advice and tips that I had really built up and tried and tested throughout the years of my experience in the blogging world.

Then, Victoria's lifestyle content has a more straightforward and understandable influence and inspiration on me and my own content. A lot of the lifestyle-themed content on InTheFrow that I have found especially idea-inducing, were about her thoughts and feelings on different 'milestones' in her life. So, this was something I really found appropriate and interesting, and that meant it was actually really easy to adapt it into my typical mental health content.

So, I started to create posts about some of my largest achievements and began picking out the anniversaries of hugely monumental events in my life to use as key themes in my content. I thoroughly enjoyed writing these pieces because I found that they provided me with some real insight into just how far my mental health had improved. Recognising my progress in my recovery was something I actually really struggled with because I was never one to blow my own trumpet.

Reading Victoria's content though, I realised that it can be so important to allow some focus on these milestones via your blog because it has a really huge potential to benefit your readers – especially where it's concerning mental health. If they're feeling hopeless and as though recovery just isn't possible, seeing you come so far can really lift their spirits and provide faith that there's the possibility of a better future. Another benefit for your readers is that if you're blogging about an anniversary of an event in your life, you'll have gained a lot of insight since it happened. This insight might end up being viewed as advice and tips for readers who may be on a similar journey/at a similar stage in their life.

Fortunately – because the content on InTheFrow isn't always relative to that which I create on I'm NOT Disordered – I'm very lucky to be able to say that one of my best-friend's; Martin Baker (Author of this Guide's foreword) actually has a mental health blog too! I think that because the events I've attended over the years haven't been targeted at bloggers (just that the hosts wanted a blogger/me there!) so I haven't had a whole lot of opportunity to meet and connect with others in this industry. Until I met Martin a good five or six years into my blogging career, though, I hadn't realised just how important and incredible it felt to have people in your life who really understand something that means the absolute world to you. I hadn't realised that because I had no one who could validate and empathise with me around blogging, I was actually having to hold back things that I wanted to say or talk about; and not having the opportunity to talk through thoughts and ideas meant that the quality of my content could be affected.

I feel that Martin's blog is really motivated and influenced by his friendship with, and care for, someone who has a mental illness, and so his content has really helped to provide me with insight into that different view point. However, even though we mostly blog from completely different angles, purely having another person who can completely comprehend what I'm thinking and feeling when I'm having a blog dilemna, has proven to be one of the most helpful aspects of having a blogger as a source for advice, inspiration, and influence.

The Unspoken Rules of Advice in Blogging

- ✓ You either take it or you leave it, and it either helps or it doesn't – there's no middle ground or grey area
- ✓ Be aware of being purposely given poor advice, driven by jealousy and/or competitiveness
- ✓ As with many scenarios, simply recognising you need advice can be a hugely important step
- ✓ Make sure you can qualify how you know what you're talking about before you start talking about it
- ✓ You might feel like a failure if the advice doesn't work for you - you're wrong. Different things work for different people
- ✓ If you think someone is taking bad advice, sometimes you have to just let them; so that they can learn it is wrong for themselves – it might mean more that way
- ✓ Be aware that some blogs are about different topics and so some advice might not even be appropriate for everyone
- ✓ Give explicit information on the advice you give in so far as to what has inspired you to give it, and who it is intended for
- ✓ Detail the goals that can practically be achieved with advice so as to avoid any disproportinate expectations
- ✓ If advice doesn't work for you, consider telling the advisor – in a nice way – to make them aware of situations where their words are unhelpful
- ✓ Keep in mind that consideration about taking your own advice, and before you speak, consider if the roles were reversed

✓ Utilise the 'search' function on Pinterest to narrow down the results to being the most appropriate for your blog

✓ Look for Facebook pages for groups of people with a common interest that ties in with your blogs theme

✓ Follow appropriate hashtags on Twitter that are intended to connect bloggers of the same subjects

✓ Google can still be your friend, but remember how important it is that blog advice comes from experience

✓ Consider using music/song lyrics that you can relate to, to help others identify with your content

✓ Don't dismiss advice from someone who you believe is bias, sometimes you need that unconditional support

✓ If you're not taking advice because you're scared of the potential result, create comfort for yourself for the aftermath and let taking the chance be less frightening

✓ Don't be arrogant and superior when giving advice, no matter how many followers you have, we all started with none

✓ If someone asks you for advice, stay humble, grateful, and honoured to know that your thoughts are trusted and appreciated

✓ Believing in karma can help you to cope if someone purposely gives you poor blogging advice

✓ If you're giving advice, do so in a way which isn't at all patronising or condescending – that will make the entire tip unappealing and render it useless immediately

✓ If your advice is asked for on one issue, don't go on to give it in places where it wasn't requested and might not be wanted

✓ The way in which you present your advice can make a huge difference to whether anyone even takes notice and tries your tips out for themselves and their own blog

My Favourite Piece of Advice For Blogging

If you've bought this Guide off the back of reading my blog (I'm NOT Disordered) or even just from following me on social media, you likely won't be surprised to hear that my most favourite nugget of advice I've ever received and found the most helpful in blogging, has been: "shy bairns get nowt!" (for anyone unfamiliar with these terms; it translates into the belief that 'if you remain shy, you won't be granted all that much in terms of opportunities etc').

It was something that came from my Mum. Sadly, I actually can't remember the first instance that she said it to me in reference to my blogging career and the various aspects and stages of it. The top and bottom of it though, is that in the first few years of I'm NOT Disordered, this advice slowly and steadily helped me to develop an increasing sense of goals and aims I was driven to achieve. In addition to this, I found myself beginning to build some high hopes for my blog's future.

Originally, I started blogging with the idea that it would be a useful means of communicating with my family and friends from the psychiatric hospital I was an inpatient in over 100 miles away from my hometown. Having just had a really productive and positive 1:1 with my Key Nurse on the ward, I felt a distinct sense of taking a huge step toward recovery; and so I also thought that blogging would be a brilliant means to document the journey for myself too. Having these two very simple and genuinly important motivations, meant that I had none of the intentions that are typical ones for new bloggers these days; in wanting to become 'famous' and have their lives be well-known, and their social media accounts and blog to be popular.

A huge reason why I didn't have those thoughts though, was because back then – in 2013 – blogging wasn't really a 'thing' and bloggers and YouTubers were only just starting to make a real name for themselves that demanded attention and some very genuine curiosity. Now that being a blogger has actually become an entire career label, those entering the industry expect a whole lot more than I ever did. That fact, sometimes leaves you wondering whether they're 'in it' for the right or the best, reasons. Almost similar to when someone joins a profession purely for the wage and not out of actual care or passion for the role/job.

I think that having a more wholesome, genuine attitude and passion around what you do – especially with blogging in particular – can really shine through the work that you do/produce and the impact it has on others. This can happen a lot with bloggers and the content created. I'd like to think that through the pieces I publish on I'm NOT Disordered, you can sense that I enjoy what I do and that I'm passionate and dedicated to everything I talk about. That I'm not mentioning an organisation or product purely because I've been rewarded in some way, to do so. There are no ulterior motives or hidden agendas in the content I publish.

Having this pure dedication and happiness for blogging, coupled with the lack of other blogs when I first entered the industry, it meant that any and all of the collaborations in those first few years were almost always a direct result of my own requests or pitches. They were always my idea – I wasn't being approached by organisations, charities, brands, companies, and well-known individuals. No one was actively hunting me down and making suggestions to work with me/my blog, and in all honesty, that felt completely warranted and actually kind of motivating in itself.

It's important to keep in mind; why would you be approached for a collaboration and be offered an opportunity or gifted something, without being established in the blogging world and holding a good reputation? It's very reasonable and understandable to recognise that the companies etc who work with bloggers are prioritising collaborating with those that have a steady standing in the digital world and which are respected by the rest of the industry.

So, having that recognition, I knew that if I wanted to feature collaborations on I'm NOT Disordered, I was going to have to go out there and get them. In recent years – now that the industry is becoming hugely over-saturated – there seems to be more and more bloggers entering this digital world, with the mistaken belief that things will automatically be handed to you on a silver platter. As though they believe that simply stating you have a blog is enough to entitle you to incredible experiences and once-in-a-lifetime opportunities. It's almost offensive to, and dismissive of, those bloggers (which, I'd like to think, includes me) who are working so hard to make their blog into something important and something worthy of others wanting to collaborate with it.

Fortunately, doing as this advice encourages and sending pitches to so many different organisations has worked massively in mine, and my blog's, favour. The amount of collaborations I've landed and the incredible nature of the ways in which I have benefited and been rewarded from them, has often been absolutely life-changing in so many different ways. So, it goes without saying that I would recommend other bloggers follow this tip – or at least take it into consideration when you're working on your blog. Especially, if you're looking to grow and develop it into something a lot bigger.

There have also been many factors, that have served as a reminder that the worst thing that could happen if I approach someone with a pitch to collaborate, is that I'll receive a "no." With my mental health being as well and stable as it is, it has meant I'm not afraid of how I'd cope with a negative response to an idea that I had put lots of thought, energy, and time into. So, I really quickly developed the belief that there was no real reason why I shouldn't follow this advice to just put yourself out there.

"You can't make decisions based on fear and the possibility of what might happen"

Michelle Obama

The Largest Blogging Decisions You Might Face

If someone were to ask me what the hardest part was about being a blogger, making decisions around my blog would definitely be the answer! It probably doesn't help that even before I started blogging, my ill mental health meant that I struggled to make really well thought-out, sensible decisions. If my mental health was poorly then I'd make decisions with the thought that the consequences of the decision wouldn't matter because I was going to commit suicide and that meant I also didn't pay much attention to the idea of there being difficult and upsetting repercussions. When my mental health was good, however, I'd always think 'life's too short!' in making decisions because I was almost 100% confident that the suicidal thoughts would come back anyway.

With my mental health improving and I'm NOT Disordered becoming so massively well-known, I found that actually, making decisions was quite a difficult process! Through my recovery, I learnt so much about responsibility and the importance of making stable, healthy decisions that were thoroughly considered and which I would be capable of coping with any of the consequences from them. That realisation, though, didn't make the pressure off knowing my decisions could be judged by so many of my blog's readers, any easier – the opposite, in fact!

All of the basics and changing them

Of course the first real decision – after deciding to blog! – is the very basic aspects of blogging such as your blog's name, the platform you'll use to host it, whether you want a personalised URL, if your blog will have a logo, if there'll be a colour scheme and strict aesthetic etc. These incredibly fundamental decisions can very understandably become hugely defining on yourself as a blogger and on your blog once it is estabilised and you begin creating content.

A lovely quality with this area requiring decisiveness, is that in those very early days – in creating the actual blog – the only real person to take into account is yourself. It can very easily be about what you would like to do with your blog; and whilst it might be important to pay some attention to the blog being attractive to others, your own opinion can fairly easily matter more. It's important to have a balance with this though; to recognise that what you find appealing might not be to everyone's taste. It means that it might be a good idea to make decisions that don't put someone off reading your blog – something more neutral and easily adaptable.

Further on in your blogging career though, when you've built up an audience and have earned avid and dedicated followers, you might reach a point where you're feeling the need to change these things up a bit and it might be a somewhat more difficult decision process.

When I first created I'm NOT Disordered, I had very little knowledge of technology – and in particular, in building a website – and so I enlisted the help of another inpatient in the psychiatric hospital I was in. So my blog wasn't exactly a huge example of impressive aesthetic or smart design; and this was especially true when she was discharged before me and I was left in a panic about who would update the layout and the 'logo.'

The logo of my blog has actually been on a massive journey of development with it originally being a ring of flowers and a photo of me in the middle… Wanting to never forget where I started on this whirlwind journey and always play homage to the humble beginnings, I've always kept the concept of the floral circle in it and so in 'design changes' it's usually about the actual 'flowers' and the colour scheme which tends to need to be tweaked to compliment their aesthetic.

The design change on I'm NOT Disordered at the end of 2022, was hugely motivated by my ten-year-long belief that continuing to have pink or purple in the logo will completely detract men from reading the blog. So, I opted for navy, black, and gold as a colour scheme and chose to still maintain the floral aspect in the logo.

Design and logo changes aren't always necessary or applicable to every blogger, I think that the reason for it to be the case with me and my blog, is because of my opinion and intention of it. I don't look at it as I had when I first created it in 2013; as a personal, private means of documenting my mental health recovery journey with the sole target audience of my family and friends and the simple intentions of improving my communication with them (they were all over 100 miles away from the psychiatric hospital I was in) and their understanding of mental illness.

I'm NOT Disordered has now, most definitely become one of the largest commitments in my life and I look at it with an incredible amount of passion and dedication. It holds responsibility for some of my most huge aspirations and long-term dreams. I hate to look at it as 'work' because surely work should be unpleasant and a resentful duty? Whereas, I find that blogging actually gives me such incredibly rewarding feelings of happiness and content, and I hold such an enormous sense of pride with it and the content I produce.

Of course, in considering changing some of the most fundamental aspects of your blog, you have to establish that you are capable of coping with the changes you're considering/planning. I have actually been pleasantly surprised to find that even with my history of struggling to cope with even the slightest aspect of change, I have managed it very well where it has been relevant to I'm NOT Disordered.

One possible reason for that is probably to do with the fact that many of the changes are made with my initiation and at my own free will. Whilst I've had reasons to make changes, I have never experienced a really firm sense of pressure to make them against my own free will. This quality is so important in switching things up on your blog because ultimately, you have to maintain a sense of your blog being yours. Ensuring that you are the one in control of it can really increase your passion and it can help to make you be more clear and decisive in making changes.

Consider featuring collaborations and guest posts

I think it's safe to say that this is a decision you'll really only start to consider when your blog is more established and you're fully invested in its content and the impact that is having on others. When you're at that stage, you might be left spending a lot of time – it could almost feel constant – thinking up ways to improve your blog and a hugely influential change on whether or not it improves, can be with the content.

When I first created I'm NOT Disordered, documenting my mental health journey was the key theme to all of my content. It was really the purpose of blogging and so, why would I pay any mind to publishing content that wasn't written by me, nor about me?

As my blog became more prominent in the industry, I began receiving tens of emails a day with positive feedback and compliments that usually took the theme of my content being helpful for a reader's own mental health. With that motivation, I began to consider whether I use I'm NOT Disordered as a platform in itself. I thought about how possible or productive it might be to begin featuring content that wasn't entirely focused on me and my own recovery. I quite liked the idea of my blog providing the opportunity for someone else to really voice their own experiences of mental health.

When my mental health first deteriorated in 2009 and I made my first suicide attempt, I literally had no friends who even remotely discussed mental illness, self-harm, or suicide. This lack of conversation gave me the impression or assumption that it wasn't a subject that should be discussed. That led to my refusal to tell anyone how I was feeling and what I was thinking at a time when, if I had done, things might not have gotten as terrible and scary as they did. So, the possibility of my blog helping others to avoid going through that – to avoid them feeling silenced – was one of the many reasons why I decided to feature guest posts.

In making the decision of using/doing collaborations on I'm NOT Disordered, it was – again – mostly about it benefiting others and not just myself. I think that because the blog posts I solely create are so helpful for me, my mental health, and my recovery; I'm more eager to provide the opportunity to experience that same notion for it to help others too.

Acknowleding that my blog could help others though used to be a process in itself because it felt like a slightly boastful thing to say. As time has gone on though, and as my blog has earned over one million readers and continued to grow and succeed for over ten years, I have felt more and more encouraged to believe that it's a completely reasonable acknowledgment. Throughout my entire blogging career I would 100% say that I have been learning constantly, and one aspect of this which I learned in recent years was that if I was to pitch a collaboration to another party, recognising that it could be beneficial for them was really important. It was actually an essential detail to securing a 'yes' from them for the proposal.

Another helpful factor in providing me with the confidence to talk about others benefiting from featuring on – or being associated with – I'm NOT Disordered, was when I first learnt about having a 'Media Kit.' Through chance, I discovered that a lot of Bloggers who like to collaborate with organisations and brands, etc have a document (which could be a PDF or saved as a PNG) where they list their achievements, previous collaboration partners, their blog's reader statistics and demographics, and the facts learnt from other similar opportunities (for example, how much increase there was in donations after working with a charity or how many items a brand sold after running an advertorial about it on your blog).

A really important aspect in deciding whether to include collaborations and guest posts is also around the potential trouble it may cause. It's essential to consider how you'll feel if whoever you collaborate with writes/submits something you aren't pleased with and which you aren't willing to put on your blog. Ideally, there really needs to be some sort of willingness to create an opportunity to discuss any disagreements or misunderstandings before making a decision to just cancel the collaboration or pull out of the project.

To have that discussion, you need to make sure that you have the right sort of relationship with the other party. For example, are you having a best-friend write a blog post about their own mental health experiences? If you are, will you be concerned for your friendship if the process of creating and publishing the guest post were to go wrong in some way? Or, are you working with a hugely public organisation and would feel intimidated being honest about your thoughts and opinions on their part of the collaboration?

Recognising that there are so many teeny tiny details – so many nooks and crannies – to a collaboration or guest post is one of the key elements for working to create and produce a successful, popular one.

The gravity of the publicity you want for your blog

When I've delivered workshops on blogging for some of my local NHS Recovery Colleges, I learnt that I always need to make it clear that a lot of the tips and advice I give, are really most important for a blog with (or which you want it to have) a large, well-known reputation. If you want your blog to remain small and not earn very much attention then some of the tips I would give – especially around attending events and featuring advertorials – just aren't that relevant or even applicable.

When I first created my blog in 2013 as a psychiatric hospital inpatient, my only target audience were my very close family and friends who were able to view my private Facebook account. To keep my blog to their attention only, I decided to share the links to my posts purely on that account.

I began blogging after a productive and hopeful 1:1 session with the Key Nurse I'd had for almost one year, because our discussion had left me feeling like it had been a real turning point that I believed was my first step on the road to recovery. After spending the previous three (almost four) years in and out of both medical and psychiatric hospitals after numerous episodes of self-harm and three suicide attempts, I really wanted to document the improvements I was making. This was partly in a bid to give them the notion of being more concrete and established, and partly to enable me to have the opportunity to look back over the journey if I began to struggle again and started to lose sight of recovery. I saw it almost as evidence that would prove I was trying so hard to get better.

In wanting to keep this journey recorded, I decided to make it somewhat public – as opposed to writing in a journal or diary – for two reasons...

Firstly, because I wanted my friends and family to be aware of what I was going through as the 127 miles distance between the hospital and home was proving to pose a challenge to maintaining effective communication. I believed that if they had a better awareness and knowledge of my experiences, then perhaps that could aid them in better supporting me both whilst in hospital, and when I was eventually (it ended up being two and a half years after being admitted!) discharged.

Secondly, I hoped that in reading my blog posts, my friends and family would feel more encouraged and empowered to speak up if they were to begin struggling with their mental health too. I thought that perhaps if they saw just how far mine had deteriorated before I finally got help, maybe it'd motivate them to do whatever they could to prevent that happening with themselves too.

Just under a year or so after creating I'm NOT Disordered, the number of readers began increasing to a level that I couldn't believe at all. I didn't understand it for a while, but then I received a number of messages from friends and then from readers who both made it clear to me that word-of-mouth was definitely working in my blog's favour! My friends and family were starting to tell others about my blog's existence and they were recommending it to people who were struggling with their own mental health in whatever way. My happiness with this wasn't centred around the fact that my number of readers was going through the roof, it was the knowledge that the more people who read my content, the more likely it was that it would actually help people.

I was also really relieved that it meant people were finally talking about mental health! When my mental health first deteriorated in some time around 2007/2009, I was immediately aware that there was literally no discussion of the topic. I don't recall there being anything in the media (though, admittedly, I was only 16/18 so maybe I didn't have full access to everything) and it certainly wasn't something my friends and family talked about. Other than for someone to tell me horror stories of our local psychiatric hospital (just years before I was admitted to it!). This silence was one of the key reasons why I didn't get help when I first started experiencing the auditory hallucinations in 2009 and is likely why they only got worse and more and more debilitating.

As the reader count climbed, I found myself feeling more and more happy when I looked at it and I began celebrating the milestones. Whilst in the psychiatric hospital, one of the other inpatients asked me why the size of my audience mattered so much. The way it was said though, wasn't out of genuine curiosity; it was more of a hint – a nod – towards the idea that holding so much importance to the statistics meant I was, in some ways, superficial.

Being asked that question for the first time; I didn't know what to say, but I had a feeling that if the trend continued and the reader count maintained the increase, then I would likely be asked the question again by someone else. That notion left me motivated to begin considering an actual answer for the next occacssion. Part of that was to have an answer, but a bigger part of it was about finding confidence in myself and validating my instincts that I wasn't blogging purely for the attention it was gaining.

So, I established that my reason for being incredibly focused on the reader count was about what that statistic actually represented. It meant that I was reaching people. That there were actual, physical people reading the posts that I was pouring my heart – and putting my everything – into. It felt rewarding to think that at least one person actually cared about what I was writing. A notion which becomes so important when you've experienced the feeling of being dismissed and ignored by mental health professionals.

The other enormous bonus of the reader count was the opportunities it earned me. As I began pitching collaboration ideas to organisations, charities, companies, and brands, it didn't take me long to recognise that if I mentioned the number of readers my blog has, it earned my pitch a lot more attention and so much more serious consideration.

Originally, I didn't really like the idea that I had to mention a statistic for a party to be interested in working with myself/ I'm NOT Disordered. Sadly, it gave me some feelings of my content being inadequate and of such a low quality that it alone, wasn't appealing or attractive and persuading enough to instil passion in the idea of a collaboration.

Admittedly, it didn't take me too long to recognise that it was actually completely understandable that the other party wouldn't want to put their effort and time into something that might be of no benefit to them. In fairness, I might have the same opinion if someone were pitching to me (which is actually the way around it mostly happens these days). Blogging, creating digital content, and writing are things which I think are hugely underestimated and so some people might be a bit surprised that you wouldn't do it just for fun rather than it needing to be seriously beneficial.

Creating content for a blog though, can be so incredibly challenging and it often takes me a good week (spending at least five hours per day) to put together a post that is the typical length of my pieces (around 3 or 4 pages on Word) and to create graphics or source images that will add appeal to the text and break it up into a less intimidating length. So, whilst I disagree with anyone who refers to my putting together a blog post as 'work' because it feels too enjoyable; I do recognise the amount of time and effort that goes into creating my blog's content. This has meant that the reader statistics sometimes feel like a reward or validating for all of those hours.

As the numbers grew into the hundreds of thousands, they motivated me to seek out collaborations and guest posts, I completely gave up on the idea of my audience being exclusive to my friends and family! It wasn't long until I found myself both really enjoying the fact that my blog was becoming so popular, and leaving behind the overwhelming and intimidating notions that came from thinking about people in totally other countries reading what I posted.

My enjoyment and pride in the thought that so many people were interested in reading the content I was creating, meant that I actually ended up taking active, passionate, and determined steps to promote the increase the publicity of my blog. Whilst I was incredibly nervous with every single media/press opportunity I took up, it felt as though there was a point to it. As though it was worthwhile; the idea that I was gaining more from these instances than I was losing in my panic and anxiety that only occurred for a short time prior to the actual interviews and filming.

One difficult consequence of the popularity of I'm NOT Disordered which actually hasn't gone anywhere despite having numerous experiences – of talking to radio hosts, BBC national news, ITV local news, my local newspaper, a magazine, a documentary – has been the thoughts and feelings of pressure. The idea that I need to be producing content that is worthwhile and deserving of all this attention. This is something I particularly struggled with when my blog was first listed as the number one Borderline Personality Disorder blog in the country.

To overcome this difficulty, I try to focus on just making sure that I continue to be happy and proud of the content I'm creating. I keep in mind that enjoying this and benefiting from this myself was the whole point of my blogging in the first place! So, whilst the increase in readers is incredibly amazing and rewarding, I need to prioritise my own opinions of I'm NOT Disordered.

How personal your content will be

Considering just how intimate and detailed your blog will be when it comes to including anything about your own life, is definitely a decision which will depend heavily upon the industry your blog fits into. It's incredibly obvious to say that a mental health blog will likely hold more personal details than a blog focused on beauty or fashion.

This aspect of being a blogger or an online influencer – that you can control just how much of 'you' that your followers see – has actually been highly controversial and a popular discussion for a number of years now. A lot of others who 'work' in the digital world and have a large following, are regularly posting on social media about the fact that their readers/subscribers/followers etc seem to make the assumption that the whole of their content is the entirety of their life. That there's nothing more important than what you've just posted online.

In all honesty, for the first few years of my blogging career – whilst I was still in the psychiatric hospital – I didn't quite agree with this stance of protest. I fully believed that I was literally blogging about everything that happened to me during that time. I talked honestly and openly about the hallucinations; the names of the voices I could hear, and the professional's explainations for the terrifying visual hallucinations of dirty rabbits completely surrounding me.

I also truthfully blogged about all of the thoughts of self-harm and the suicidal feelings that I experienced and tackled on a regular (though it felt constant at the time) basis. In addition to talking about when I was struggling, I also wrote about the actual instances of self-harm, and my four suicide attempts, and being sedated, and being restrained, and being put on life support... I felt as though if I didn't talk about these things then I would end up completely engulfed by all of this darkness and chaos and I'd drown in it. If there was no relief from all of this hurt and upset then it was just going to build up inside of me until I exploded – and I was terrified to think of the damage I would inflict on myself if that were to happen.

I was able to be so honest and open because I had spent the previous three or four years keeping my illness a secret from all of my friends and I had grown so tired of that. I was tired of all the things I had to do to maintain the lies I was telling and when it came to being admitted to a psychiatric hospital that stated the average length of admission was '12 – 18 months,' I had desperately searched my head for excuses and ways I could explain away my absence. In the end though, I admitted defeat and disclosed the situation in a Facebook post which earned a lot of love and support from my friends.

So, having had that positive experience of being honest, and the memories of how difficult it was to cover up the truth, I wasn't ever that scared or anxious at the thought of the response my honesty in my blog posts might earn me. Except for one post... In September 2013, I made a number of threatening comments to a member of staff in the hospital after she had made a remark on the abuse I had experienced when I was younger.

What she said had been wrong – she shouldn't have said it and could have gotten into actual, serious trouble for it – but, my response and behaviour rendered her comment slightly less terrible. It was similar to when people talk about sinking to someone's level; I had made numerous threats that could admittedly be very easily be viewed as a whole lot more deplorable than her one comment. Until that instance, I was actually proud that I hadn't ever been aggressive towards staff, but with this, I ended up (after talking it through with others) feeling regretful and ashamed of what I had said.

My honestly, very real urge to backtrack and massively apologise for everything I had said, left me incredibly reluctant to actually blog about the incident. I was worried that readers would have the opinion or belief that this was an example of the 'real me' in that they'd think less of my as a person. I also believed that there'd be some people out there who might use it as an example to solidify the stigma held against those with a mental illness which labelled the person with a diagnosis as violent or even just a terrible person in general.

In the end, however, I decided to write about the incident because I would rather be judged for something I have done than someone hold an opinion of me purely because of my diagnosis, self-harm, suicide attempts, or mental health in general. I think that making that decision was quite a pivotal moment in my thought process around considering what to make public knowledge and what not to.

In making those decisions, I usually just use my gut instinct and go with whatever feels 'right' or whatever I think will help the most people. I do so because I don't think that asking for someone else's opinion on whether or not to disclose a particular instance on my blog, is kind of defeating the purpose.

Also, the one person I might have asked – the most important person in my life (my Mum) – is a very private person and she, herself, carefully chooses when, where, and who to divulge information to. So, whilst she's incredibly supportive and a massive promoter of my blogging, I don't think it'd be right to ask her view if I was struggling to decide whether to write about something by myself. There have been instances where I have done a role reversal and where my Mum was silent, I might have said something; and so I don't know if my Mum would experience that conflict too. I'd like to think though, that despite that difference, we have such a strong connection that means I respect her decisions and she respects mine, and we both acknowledge and support what is right for each other.

As the years have gone by, though, I've come across a number of instances in my life where I've been faced with the decision as to whether or not to make it public knowledge. In these moments, I've made my mind up by considering whether talking about it on my blog will benefit myself and/or my readers. If I'd find it helpful and therapeutic to talk about it and think of it as a way to process my thoughts and feelings around something, then I consider it to be worth blogging about it. Or, if it will reassure others that they aren't alone if they've experienced something similar, and bring them hope that you can come through it; then that would lead me to think that it was worthwhile making it public knowledge.

5 Ways To Cope With Trying To Make A Decision

No matter what your mental state is, no matter what your mental health history is, no matter what the decision is for/on, no matter how quickly you have to make it, no matter how important it is…

Making a decision can be challenging!

Even the ones that feel straight forward and almost automatic – there's always the chance it will be difficult to cope with the entire decision making process. Struggling with this can be really debilitating because it has the potential to result in a knock to your confidence and can end up having an impact on the actual decision.

So here are five quick tips to prevent this from happening…

1. Utilise a Pro's and Con's lists to ensure your decision is balanced and free from emotion and impulsivity
2. Talk your thought process through with others to ensure there's no bias or self-centred nature to the decision
3. Be careful not to confuse taking responsibility for the consequences of your decision and blaming yourself if it's a bad result
4. Consider any advice you'd give others if the situation were reversed so as to avoid any disproportionate responsibility
5. If you're starting to feel stressed and frazzled, utilise self-soothing activities e.g. take a bath or go for a walk

The Big Blogging Decision That I Went Back On

In September 2014, with my discharge from the psychiatric hospital scheduled to be within a week, I created a post on I'm NOT Disordered asking for the thoughts of others. I was considering whether my discharge should mean the end of my blogging career.

When I first created my blog in January 2013, I did so with many intentions and hopes. The largest goal though, was to improve the knowledge and understanding of my friends and family, who I was struggling to communicate with because the hospital was 127 miles away from all of them.

Growing up, I had no real education around mental health and my memory which most resembles that, is of someone telling me 'horror stories' of my local psychiatric hospital when we drove past it. Other than that though, I can't remember ever even seeing anything about the topic in the media I had access to. Having such little information about mental health meant that when I was sectioned under the 1983 Mental Health Act and admitted to that local hospital, my head was filled with visions of those horror stories coming true.

There was also no one in my life who ever talked about mental health and the absence of having such productive and educational conversations meant that when my mental health deteriorated in 2009, and I started to hear voices; I kept silent for almost two weeks. Looking back, I wonder whether things would have gotten to the point they did if I had felt capable or encouraged to get help and to talk to someone straight away.

The lack of understanding of the reality of mental health and psychiatric hospitals and the uncertainty around speaking about my mental illness, spurred me on in my blogging. They gave me the great sense that I wouldn't be alone in that; that there were others both in my life, and out of it, that didn't understand mental health and who felt sceptical and hesitant of talking about their own experiences of it too. This resolve, left me with a passion and drive to use my own difficulties as a source for discouraging it.

I think that the absence of nervousness and anxiety at the thought of the response I/my blog might get in talking about my mental health so honestly and openly, was largely down to me having the notion that my life couldn't possibly get any worse. I had gone through the traumatic abuse, I had been on life support after a suicide attempt, I was detained in a secure hospital that was over 100 miles away from home, and I was being instructed to undergo Therapy and take medication! It left me questioning – if I kept perspective – exactly how much (if any) difference it would make to my mood if I were to receive online abuse...

Beginning, I'm NOT Disordered as a psychiatric inpatient also meant two things:

1. There was always something happening and therefore always something to blog about!
2. For the best part of my blog's existence, my content was more about my poor mental health than positivity

With these two factors in mind, I'd like to think it is more than understandable – and almost predictable – to know that when my discharge was being planned, I would consider closing my blog down. It was, firstly, about the idea of moving into my own home in the community like a 'normal person,' which left me sceptical that anything would happen in my life that was worthy of being written about; let alone actually publicised. This also meant, though, that to finally be discharged from the psychiatric hospital after two and a half years (with around one and a half of them featuring on my blog) would only happen when my mental health was in recovery and I was safe and stable. So, not only did I believe that my life would be uneventful, I also thought that if I wasn't suicdal or having urges to self-harm or experiencing hallucinations or memories of the trauma, why would I need to write about anything for me own therapeutic benefit?

Not long after I wrote a piece on I'm NOT Disordered on September 8th which was titled: 'A Massive Decision (That I Shouldn't Make Alone),' I went on to create content for World Suicide Prevention Day 2014. I decided to quickly talk about the three suicide attempts I had made up to that point, and explained that I was doing so to illustrate that as sure as I was that everything was hopeless and I'd never get better; things did – and I did! I wanted them to give people hope.

However, not every reader is there for a positive reason. Not everyone reads blogs with an eager and interested outlook and on positive motivations. Some come along with bad intentions and a negative view of the subjects being blogged about. So, I received a comment on my Prevention Day piece which encouraged me to have a 'fourth attempt' and wishing me 'luck' with it. I just remember reading it and my mouth dropping open as tears almost instantly pricked at my eyes. I felt drowned in the overwhelming notion that my post had been worthless.

There's a lot of things that go on 'behind-the-scenes' in blogging – things that so many readers and people outside of the industry have absolutely no idea about. One of these unseen elements, is the toll putting together content takes on the blogger. I think that sometimes readers or friends and family of a blogger can really see the dedicaiton, time, effort, and passion that a blogger is putting into their content; but that's completely different to what I'm talking about. I think that it's incredibly understandable for people to assume that because I blog about mental health so frequently, it mustn't be too challenging – especially not after ten years of doing this. But it is. I'm telling you, it is.

So, when I write about suicide attempts – as I did in this post in September 2014 – it can take a lot out of me because I really feel as though I'm putting so much of myself into content like that. It feels like I'm baring my soul. You know, so many people say that once you put your life out there online and on social media, you make yourself vulnerable. Vulernable to bullying, to obsession, to judgment etc. I continued to make myself open to all of these dangers and results that can come from blogging, because I honestly and completely felt that the benefits I was (and, according to emails, feedback, and comments; others were too) receiving from it, made it totally worth the risk.

Despite taking a concious decision to blog despite these possible dangers, that doesn't take away how upset I felt when I received that comment about making a fourth attempt... In fact, it was almost more upsetting than I imagine it being had I gone into things naiive and blindsided because receiving something this nasty after feeling that you've made a responsible and reliable decision to face the possibility of it happening, can feel so completely debilitating and can come as a massive knock to your confidence. How can you deem your decisions to be accurate any more?

Following the Suicide Prevention Day post with the horrible comment, I was left completely confident that ending I'm NOT Disordered was the right move; and the following post on September 12th 2014 was actually titled; 'The End of I'm NOT Disordered.' In the post, I wrote about my recognition that this comment hadn't been mental health stigma related; it wasn't about someone having a lack of understanding, education, or information on the issue at hand, it was purely bullying. So, it felt as though there was nothing I could do to change it – I couldn't provide more experience and knowledge to teach people to have better empathy and awareness of how their comments can affect a person's mental health. The spiteful comment wasn't about that.

So, from September 12th until October 29th 2014, I lived a life that wasn't shared on I'm NOT Disordered. In the blog post on my return to the industry (on the 29th) I titled it; 'An Explanation' and used it as an opportunity to do just that – explain.

I talked about how I found myself having experiences and 'life events' where I've almost automatically had the thought to blog about it. I felt certain that documenting things would help me both process it and relish in it. As though as well as finding it therapeutic to write about it and the thoughts and feelings I was experiencing, I would also benefit from blogging about something because it would let me really acknowledge it and document it in a way that would solidify it as a memory.

In the explanation post, I also talked about having the realisation that it could be really important to acknowledge your past and to really own it as being a part of why your present is the way it is. I had grown to like the idea of looking at the blog posts I'd written back in the years I was in the psychiatric hospital and putting them alongside these new posts about my journey in my own home in the community, just a ten minute walk from my Mum's house.

I think that the real catalyst for these two changes in my perspective, was the realisation that mental health recovery isn't the linear journey that so many psychiatric professionals and others proclaim or assume it to be. Being discharged from hospital was made it to sound as though it could only be reached if your mental health completely stabilised and you were 100% safe for 100% of the time. It really shouldn't have taken me learning that this just wasn't the truth the hard way in me self-harming for the first time after my discharge. I should have been warned that it could be that way. That there was every chance that your 'recovery' would be a whole journey of highs and lows and that sometimes being out of hospital wasn't so much about guaranteeing your safety more than it was recognising you have the ability to cope with any upset and difficult thoughts and feelings in a much healthier way.

With recovery not being all that I felt it was advertised as being, I felt that I owed it to all the other mental health service users who are being encouraged to work towards this false ideal future, to tell them the truth. I honestly believe that if I'd been warned that this was recovery, I definitely wouldn't have cried hysterically and been convinced that 'everything was ruined' and I was going to be admitted back into hospital. Instead, I would have felt prepared and would have had even the most mildest idea of how to cope with it. Something, which I believed that all mental health service users should be granted and worthy of.

Writing that blog post after vowing to end the blog and keeping a silence lasting over one month, I won't lie – it felt really awkward and difficult! It's actually something that others do that really grates on me! When people will say on social media that they're ending their account and then they're back posting within hours or days!

I'd also say that I'm quite a proud person and I definitely enjoy being 'right' about things. So, to have to go back on my word? It was a concept I struggled with, and having to do it so publicly (at that point, I'm NOT Disordered had a few thousand readers)? That just made everything all the more challenging. However, I was certain that it was going to be worth it because I fully believed that I was making the right decision.

The Ultimate Rule of Blog Decisions

Ensure there's a balance between what your readers want and what you want

Making a decision can be one of the most uncertain, difficult, chaotic, and tumultuous moments in your blogging career. Most blogs are ran by an individual and not a number of people creating content collaboratively; so when a blog faces a crossroads, it typically falls upon the head of one person to make that final call.

This means, that one person can have an enormously, huge amount of responsibility in their blogging career – not just during the decision-making process, but also in the aftermath too. I believe that this is one of those situations where a stubborn, unsupportive person could turn around and say "you got yourself into it..." As though choosing to do something means you're completely aware of, and have chosen to fully committed to, absolutely all of the challenges it might entail. Almost as if job descriptions are completely accurate and literally nothing is left out or forgotten! A role we take on, isn't always about what you 'signed up for.'

So, in being a blogger you are almost inevitably faced with numerous forms of decisions around your blog – with each competing against the next in how important and difficult they are. This can seem overwhelming – especially in the beginning of your blogging days because that's the point when there are so many decisions to be made. Decisions which can really shape the entire path and journey of your blog and which can lend themselves as impactful upon your blog's success and popularity.

So, with the idea of how challenging they can be coupled with the fact bloggers will typically face the decision alone, it can be so meaningful to have some sort of guidance to look to when you're in this situation. In the early days of I'm NOT Disordered, when I was faced with a difficult fork in the road, I went with my heart and my gut. I opted for the decision that felt the most 'right' and which I felt happier and more content with. I think that in doing things this way, it left me feeling more responsible for whatever results and consequences came from the decision.

Shortly after the reader count hit the hundreds of thousands, I came across an uncertainty in an instance where I need to make a decision. I began taking a lot more time, and putting a lot more effort, into my decisions. I think that a lot of that extra consideration was mostly due to the notion of there being a much more heightened level of pressure that can come with the notion of the larger your following, the more people you may feel the need and desire to impress.

It actually didn't take me too long to recognise that I was putting a lot of stress on myself and spending far too much time concentrating on my readers and their expectations and needs of my blog, rather than my own. The way I quickly learnt this though, was because I found myself feeling less and less passionate about blogging. I stopped enjoying putting the content together so much and I lost all excitement when I was publishing posts and no longer felt anticipation and eagerness to see the response my work got.

I realised quickly that I was no longer blogging for myself and that almost immediately saddened me. So, I reminded myself of why I'd created I'm NOT Disordered in the first place... That it was about me and it was equally about my readers (even though back then my target audience was my friends and family). It was about providing my readers with a better understanding of mental health. It was about me feeling more confident and less ashamed of talking about my mental health. It was about encouraging others not to feel alone and to inspire them to speak up too.

Another means of recognising my deterioration in my motivation and enjoyment around blogging, was the notion that there'd been a bit of a lull in I'm NOT Disordered's statistics around its popularity. It made me wonder whether my loss of morale had reflected upon my content and whether readers had picked up on that.

So my love of seeing my blog reach more and more people, coupled with the loss of passion, led me to making a concious effort to bring balance to things. To really ensure there was a balance between my readers thoughts and feelings about my blog and my own. I tried to always keep in mind that we are all equally important to the functioning of the blog. I mean, I could write posts and posts, but if no one ever saw them, what would be the point in me doing a blog and not just keeping a diary?

I was asked once why I cared so much about the number of readers my blog is gaining, and the person asking wasn't asking in a genuinely curious way. She meant it as a jibe at the idea that I'm materialistic and shallow, and that I'm in this industry for all the wrong reasons. At the time, it was only a few months into my blogging career and the question wasn't something I had been asked before or which I'd asked of myself! Which meant that I hadn't been able to have the time to consider my answer to it and to mull over how to phrase things.

Now, though, it is ten years since I started blogging, and I've discovered that I have a number of reasons why I care about the reader count. The two largest of these reasons though, are firstly that each number reflects one person who my content has the possibility of helping in some way. The idea that my words can be of some sort of benefit for someone reading, feels so rewarding and is such a positive for my own mental health too. It leaves me with the notion that all that I have gone thorugh has been worthwhile if I can use it to help someone else.

Secondly, I've really found comfort and happiness in the fact that the higher the audience number, the higher the chance of me landing the amazing opportunities, event invitations, gifted items, and collaborations that I have had over the years (since being about 2 or 3 years into my blogging career). Sometimes, this fact makes me saddened, because surely these sorts of succeses should be a direct result of the quality of your content? However, you could turn this on its head, and argue that your blog wouldn't have as many readers if the quality of your content wasn't up to par.

Either way though, the recognition that I appreciated every single one of I'm NOT Disordered's readers gave me a clue as to why I was so often prioritising them when making any sort of decisions around the blog. This, and seeing how much my passion and enjoyment dwindled when I wasn't doing things the way I wanted to, really helped me in deciding that finding a balance was the right way to go. So, I try to look at decisions by thinking up a few of the routes I'd like to take, and then considering how beneficial each would be for my readers and picking that option. It means that even whilst I'm prioritising myself and my own thoughts and opinions on this blog that I have so many years working on, I'm also recognising that the readers who have really helped make it what it is today, seriously matter and hold a huge level of importance.

"In life, I regret the things I didn't do far more than the missteps I made along the way"

David Stanley

Why It Helps To Deem Regrets As Learning Curves

In considering making decisions and taking on advice, it almost naturally feeds into a discussion on regrets and instances which you wish you could take back and do it all over again completely differently.

Growing up, I was so innocent and naïve (something which I think – to a degree – is a good quality to have in a childhood) and had absolutely no education or understanding of mental health/illness. It meant that as I got older, I was firstly horrified and shocked to discover there were such bad people in the world as the person who abused and raped me when I was in my teens (15-16). I didn't even know the names for what was being done to me since the only sexual education I'd had was putting a condom on a banana! It meant that my only real knowledge or certainty that what was happening was wrong and bad, was that it almost naturally and immediately felt that way.

Then, when my mental health deteriorated and I began hearing auditory hallucinations in the form of voices, I was absolutely stunned into silence. I didn't realise that it didn't make me instantly 'crazy' or mean that people in white coats would cart me off to the local psychiatric hospital and hold me down while giving me electric shocks as I screamed for help!

These two areas where I lacked understanding, meant my loss of education was almost fatal. When my attempt to report the abuse to my abuser's boss left me labelled a liar; I had no idea I had the right to go to the Police, and so I held my tongue for another two years. Then, I also didn't get help from my doctor as soon as the voices started and when the suicidal thoughts were growing stronger. Keeping these enormous life-changing events quiet, meant that I was almost constantly on tiptoes in my life. I was convinced that one gentle nudge in the wrong (depending on how you look at it) direction would tip me over the edge! I knew that if someone upset me or argued with me over something, I might lose all will and determination not to make a suicide attempt or to self-harm. Thing was, because no one knew what had happened, no one knew to be on their tiptoes too! So, when my weekend job got stressful, it really knocked me and ten days later, I found myself making my first suicide attempt.

Being 18 when I made the attempt, meant that I could be detained under the 1983 Mental Health Act, and when I was; it meant that I was put into the adult mental health system and had missed any sort of steady progression from children's services etc. So, walking into that psychiatric hospital for the first time, I remember struggling to put one foot in front of the other because my legs were shaking so badly, and they didn't want to move forward!

This became my first notion of regret. The recognition that the absence of education, knowledge, and understanding of abuse and mental health played hugely important roles in just how terrible everything got, made it incredibly difficult to not look at these things as regretful.

For the three or four years following this established first regret, I spent the time literally building on that and adding more and more regrets to the pile. It seemed as though every day, I was putting myself in a situation that never ended well. I would run away, I'd self-harm, I'd be admitted to hospital, I'd stop eating...

In all honesty though, I really didn't see how high that pile of regrets was until about a year into my psychiatric hospital admission/a month or so into my blogging career. It was right around the time when I started to realise that recovery was actually really possible, and just as quick as that hit me, I had the memories of all those regrets shot at me and I struggled to not take a step backwards. It very easily let me see that if I couldn't find a way to live with – or at the very least, be able to cope with – these 'regrets' then I might never truly 'recover.' So, I began cooperating and really devoting myself to working with the staff in finding coping strategies and learning skills to cope with 'regrets' in a more positive and safe way.

Whilst therapy and chats with the psychiatric hospital staff taught me how to live alongside these difficult and resented thoughts and memories, when I was discharged after a further 18 months, I found myself struggling again. Since I hadn't really combatted the 'regrets,' they were still there in the background and it meant that when I was vulnerable and upset over something, I was more prone to still struggling with them.

So, because of this continued possibility of me fighting the thoughts and feelings that come alongside any actions you've taken that you resent and wish you hadn't, I ended up seeing the Crisis Team. They gave me the most useful piece of advice I think I've ever had since leaving the hospital in 2014; they told me that "as long as you learn something – anything – from a 'mistake,' it was worth making it!" Hearing that little motto/thought process was like a refreshing sentence that seemed to almost automatically make sense and fitted with my own aims, goals, and thoughts and feelings about things.

Fortunately, being taught this important lesson, came at the right time in so far as my blogging career because it was around the years when I began taking my work/content on I'm NOT Disordered really seriously. Even though, almost straight away after I started blogging, I had the recognition that I'd found a purpose – something which was such a lovely and reassuring notion after spending years convinced that I was literally, purely destined to kill myself – it actually took a little while for it to feel more long-term and important.

You're NOT Disordered

I think that the reason it took some time, was because for the first two or three years of blogging, I didn't imagine that it would continue for much longer – I definitely didn't think that it would get to the point of being ten years (as it reached in January 2023)! With professionals either outright claiming – or alluding to – the idea that recovery is linear and once you've reached it, there'll never be a bad day; I felt fairly confident that I wouldn't need my blog for any length of time beyond my discharge from the psychiatric hospital. So, it felt as though yes, I had found a purpose, but that it was about reaching recovery and it not still being the case nine years after being discharged. I didn't expect it to become one of the most important and defining elements in my life.

Establishing how meaningful and essential I'm NOT Disordered is for me meant I became so much more invested in it, and that had one downside. It meant that if I did anything with or for my blog that I felt turned out to be a 'mistake' or which I 'regretted,' it meant a whole lot more to me and so it had a larger, more negative impact on my mental health. I regarded anything I deemed to be errors in judgment around the content I created or the design changes I made to my blog, to a higher level of importance.

Doing this, meant that it was almost instantly really essential that I have a way to cope with these thoughts and feelings of failure and disappointment. This was because – as we all know – mental health recovery isn't about everything being perfect 100% of the time! So, regardless of the fact that I had my own home and that I was on medication, there was every chance that I might end up coping with difficult emotions in an unsafe way again. So, I turned to the advice of the Crisis Team, and I saw these issues as learning opportunities and the chance to gain insight and experience that wasn't wholly bad or wrong.

A Blogging Lesson I Wish I'd Learnt Sooner

Alongside and similarly to the prospect of regretful decisions in your blog career, another difficult thought or emotion you might experience is around the chance of learning something and finding yourself mulling over the fact that you wish you had learnt it so much earlier in your blogging journey.

Something I've been confident of for quite a long time now, is that I've definitely learnt things the hard way over the years of my blogging career. I think that because I created, I'm NOT Disordered in 2013, at a time when there were really only three well-known mental health blogs (and none of them were written by a psychiatric hospital inpatient – as I was then), there was no mental health blogger to really 'lead the way' for me.

The absence of a role model was actually something that I also struggled with when my mental health was really poorly. The fact that no one in my life ever spoke about mental health or showed any obvious signs of struggling with their own, meant that I felt there was no one to turn to as a means of identifying over a mutual difficulty. This also meant the loss of having someone to look up to and to help me to create a goal or an ideal as to what to work towards for my recovery.

So, without that, I found myself trusting my instincts... But, at first, a lot of my 'instincts' during my mental illness were almost completely and incredibly negative or unsafe. I nearly always believed that the 'right' way to cope with anything challenging that arose in my life, was to hold myself responsible and to then inflict some sort of punishment (usually self-harm). Fortunately, despite everyone I came to know or consider a friend in mental health being a mostly negative inspiration, I found a goal for recovery by myself, when I started blogging. The simple and incredibly encouraging notion that I'd found a purpose in life by creating I'm NOT Disordered gave me the motivation I needed to feel positive about the thought of recovery. It left me wanting to continue with this and strive to build a huge, exciting, and powerful future for my blog.

So, that helped with my journey to recovery, but I was then faced with the similar dilemma on my blog in that because there weren't many mental health blogs at that time, I was without a role model. Again, without that person or direct influence, I was sort of stumbling around in the dark. I was just feeling my way through the first few months; purely acting on my own thoughts and feelings of what was the right move or the right next step for my blog. I trusted my new, positive, and productive instincts.

As time has gone by though, I've found my creativity has become helpful in leading me to think up and discover influences and inspiration in more unique and random ways. Which is when and why I turned to Victoria Magrath from the primarily fashion and beauty (though she often includes lifestyle and travel content too) blog 'InTheFrow.' Despite her posts largely being of a, perhaps dissimilar and irrelevant, theme and angle to my own; I found her passion, dedication, and general work ethic really inspirational. I've found it incredible to see the way she seems to never settle in that once she's achieved something, she doesn't rest back on her laurels – she just dreams bigger and works harder.

Finally finding some sort of role model in blogging, gave me the ability to gain insight into aspects of this industry that I was yet to face e.g., collaborations, speaking with the press, featuring in the media, and being given free items and products in return for publicity. This meant that not only was I granted the opportunity to learn more about blogging before it was thrown upon me, but

I also had someone to turn to for guidance and inspiration when I was facing challenges that I had no clue about.

Fortunately for this aspect of blogging, I actually really enjoy learning new things, so even where I came against something that hinted that some lengthy reading would be favoured/recommended, I was excited about it! It likely also helped that I was so passionate and dedicated to creating content and doing all that I could to improve I'm NOT Disordered because it meant I was more committed and willing to go to the extra lengths that were sometimes necessary in order to make any changes that I wanted or in order to tackle any problems and overcome any forks in the road.

Having that passion, though, isn't exactly a magic key to things – it means I'm more willing to learn, but it doesn't make learning lessons around blogging any more simple or any less confusing. I would still sum up the learning curves I've experienced as me having to learn things 'the hard way.' This, however, has become a whole new motivation for me to continue blogging and has actually also directly inspired some content because I've been filled with the notion that I wanted to do all that I could to help other bloggers avoid having to learn these things in the most difficult, inconsiderate, encompassing, inconvenient, and chaotic way! I do this out of fear that someone who has a huge potential to go far in their blogging career and to do so much good with their content, will be thrown off by the challenges that come with a lack of knowledge, education, information, and understanding of things.

So, I thought it might be interesting to use part of this Guide as a means for confronting one of the largest learning curves that I've conquered in my blogging career, but which I do wish I had known about sooner so that my blog could have been of a higher standard from the beginning... Altering my blog's design.

I think there are many common misconceptions in the blogging industry, but one which is really relevant here is that a large amount of people will assume that a blogger has hugely impressive skills in technology. It's as though outsiders think that running a blog requires advanced technical education in computers and the digital world in general; and I do completely recognise the rationale behind thought even though I've never experienced it. It wasn't even as though I was hesitant to begin blogging because I feared that I was too uneducated in that industry – which, I think, is a frequent experience for a lot of people who end up pushing the idea of blogging to one side.

The fact that I created I'm NOT Disordered in 2013 when there was a huge lack of mental health blogs out there, ended up meaning a lot in regard to this learning curve. Firstly, it meant that there were few sources of design inspiration and therefore no real air of competition so as to motivate any ideas and decisions around the colour scheme, the logo, the layout, and general aesthetics of my blog. There was no standard set nor a bar being raised to encourage refreshes and updates of these elements of your blog.

Secondly, the fact there were so few mental health blogs also meant that there was no really huge resources for education around the technical aspects that you need to have knowledge of in order to make some of the largest design changes. It wasn't like these days where I can check on my favourite blogs, see an aesthetic detail I find inspirational or which I would like to tweak and then feature on I'm NOT Disordered, and be able to simply Google how to do that. In 2013, it was more about purely following my own likes and dislikes for the appearance of my blog.

For the first year or so, that way of working was absolutely fine because for the most part of that time, my target audience was purely my friends and family. I felt that this meant there was no real essential need or notion of necessity for my blog's design to be appealing and aesthetically pleasing. For that length of time, I didn't experience any sense of pressure or even motivation to tweak anything around the layout or colour scheme of the blog.

When – after just over a year – word of mouth publicity began to lead my blog statistics to really 'take off' and the size of my audience came nearer and nearer to the hundreds of thousands; I found myself starting to put a lot of time, effort, and consideration into my blog's appearance. Having so many readers made me convinced that I'm NOT Disordered really needed to earn and be worthy of all of that attention; and aside from my content, I thought the other way to do that would be in having an amazing design.

I also recognised that with a larger audience and a very universal topic, my blog really needed to be appealing for everyone and I worried that if I continued to feature so much of my favourite colour of pink and the flower illustrations I loved, then it could be unattractive to a whole host of other people! Plus, with my mission in blogging to be that I wanted to help others with their mental health, I felt an eagerness to have a design that is pleasing for as many people as possible in order to do that.

In the few huge aesthetic changes, I've made to my blog, I've tried to always play some sort of homage to my blog's beginning by maintaining some sort of floral aspect to the blog's design/graphics/logo. Despite how much I feel my content has improved since I started creating posts, I'm forever proud of where this all began. I'd like to think that because of my mental illness and suicide attempts, I'm really very grateful for the smallest of things in life now, and this means feeling appreciative of that small beginning.

How did I'm NOT Disordered, and I get from there to where we are now? Google, Canva, and Pipdig! When I first started blogging, I was in the psychiatric hospital and the girl I was close to there was quite good with computers and so she actually helped me a lot in bringing my ideas to life. Except they started talking about discharging her way before I would be, and I realised I really needed to learn how to do these things by myself because I didn't want to have to message her and wait for a response every time I wanted to tweak something. I wanted to be in control.

So, Google became my best friend, and I searched high and low for instructions on how to make the changes I wanted to make. These searches led me to finding Pipdig who are now my blog's design company. Pipdig are an online service where you can purchase (for very reasonable prices) templates to format and present your blog's layout and design. I was terrified initially because it was all about coding and despite having been blogging for a number of years by this point, I still wasn't familiar with that side of it.

Then, a number of years ago, I completed a Digital Marketing Internship where I learnt so much about a huge number of new elements in the digital world – whether that be across social media or actual websites. I learnt a lot of technical language, what those things mean, and how you could utilise them to give my blog (though I was learning them for a company's website) a boost and improve its chance of being successful. It was in the Internship that I learnt about Canva.

Canva is a website that provides the chance to create really advanced and impressive graphics or documents of any sort – from leaflets to social media banners to photo collages to CV's! Despite all I learnt in the Internship, I still believe that every time I create something on Canva, I find out something new about it – new function or a different method to create a blog title graphic etc. I feel that it's really brought my blog and its content to life, and it's given a more appealing and attractive finish to the posts.

"We are what we pretend to be, so we must be careful about what we pretend to be"

Kurt Vonnegut

A Discussion on Disclosure

Fortunately, I was one of the very few inpatients in the psychiatric hospital who had the same Named Nurse throughout my admissions (all two-and-a-half years of it!). So, it meant we built and created a really important and therapeutic relationship that meant we had so many productive and helpful 1:1 conversations.

On January 6th 2013, we had one of those really useful discussions after I had begun experiencing flashbacks to parts of the abuse I had experienced that I hadn't told anyone about. My silence and reluctance to really talk through these instances meant that when the ward staff were trying to 'help' or 'support' me, they weren't getting it right. So, my Named Nurse and I agreed to create a care plan detailing that every night I would write something about the abuse and give it to the staff to read in a bid to improve their understanding and my care and progress my recovery.

This 1:1 and the arrangement ended up being such a positive and productive step in the 'right' direction that I wanted to document the progress and so, I created I'm NOT Disordered and began blogging! It was such a spontaneous – but obviously very good – decision that I didn't think of all the complications that might come with suddenly sharing my journey through my mental illness with others. With my initial target audience being my family and friends on my private Facebook account, though, it meant that I wasn't too thrown, in regard to deciding how much detail I should share.

For the three years prior to the admission in 2012, I worked really hard to keep my mental illness and associating 'symptoms' a huge secret from almost everyone in my life. I wore large bracelets on nights out to cover self-harm scars/wounds and as things escalated, I began wearing long sleeved tops. When I had to cancel plans with friends because I was in hospital, I would either flat out lie or tell them I was in hospital for something medical and not that I'd made another suicide attempt or had been hallucinating.

Back then, mental health really wasn't spoken about a whole lot – or at least not to an extent where I was aware of it before I became poorly. I heard horror stories of our local psychiatric hospital and if I heard someone hallucinated my first word would have been "crazy!" I don't recall ever seeing anything in all the media that I had access to at that age (18), nor was there any education in school around mental health. This absence of knowledge or an accurate understanding meant that I was embarrassed when I began struggling and so I didn't get help as soon as I became unwell. I'll never know whether if I had done, things would have gotten to the point they did.

When the decision was made to section me to a psychiatric hospital where the 'average length of admission' was stated as being 12 – 18 months, I wracked my brains trying desperately to think of a lie to excuse myself from my social circle. Eventually, I came to the conclusion that I would be honest and so I posted a status on Facebook stating that due to the stigma surrounding mental health, I hadn't felt able to speak up sooner, but now I needed to. I was incredibly surprised to receive an absolute ton of lovely and supportive comments from my family and friends who all illustrated unconditional support for me. I actually ended up feeling absolutely shameful for even just imagining I would get any other response from these most amazing people in my life.

That disclosure actually became a really good encouragement and inspiration when it came to finally starting to blog. It kind of bolstered me into some moderate level of reassurance that I could be fairly open and honest when it came to the level of detail, I gave around my mental health... and everything that came with it! Alongside that though, there was also a poorly part of me who didn't care all that much about what people knew, how they knew, and when they knew it! That part sort of had the thought that "why should I keep suffering in silence for the sake of worrying about how everyone else will feel?!" It was almost ironic that this was a difficult thought, but it actually was good news because it meant that I finally recognised the importance of putting myself first and doing what was best for my mental health rather than worrying about the reactions of others.

This new-found way of life made all the difference in those early stages of my blogging career as I found myself fully able to appreciate that honesty really was the best policy in mental health. This meant that when my blog's readership began to really grow, I quickly discovered that my honesty was inspiring others to do the same. I'm NOT Disordered was actually beginning to help others in addition to myself.

Of course, everything comes with their ups and downs and a big challenge in being so open and – at most times – just really brutally honest, was my readers perception that this was my entire life. That the content on my blog was just all that there was to me. As though I'm being open, I was baring my soul and telling my entire life story!

Fortunately, I completely appreciated that thought process because at some point, I found myself falling into the trap of that way of thinking when talking about the bloggers I follow too. It's almost easy to just assume that a person seemingly posting lots of details of their life isn't holding anything back – their dog is always frolicking in a field, or their makeup is always on point, or their home is always neat and tidy! As though nothing is ever out of place.

With a truthful, open mental health blog, however, it's a bit of a different story and even more easily and understandably misleading because the reader is seeing the good and the bad and so what could there possibly be left that you're not telling them?! It's almost more straightforward to find yourself convinced that you know the blogger's life story and all the darkest, most brutal ins and outs of their journey as well as their incredibly high achievements or monumental moments.

The issue of disclosing details about your life on your blog can sometimes lead to the question: "what's the point of blogging if you're only in it halfway?" As though if you're not fully dedicated and willing to talk about everything going on for you, there's no real purpose in having a blog. In fairness, I'd say that you do really – if you want to make 'something' of your blog – need to be 'all in' with this industry.

Aside from readers assuming they know everything, a challenge that I've found with disclosure that is perhaps more personal for me, is that my family members are actually quite private people. This is particularly difficult and relevant with my Mum, who I'm incredibly close to and who means a great deal – especially to my mental health. Her unconditional love and support are so appreciated and have truly been lifesaving at times, but there's been a lot of things in our journey together that I've been unable to talk about on my blog because my Mum has requested that they remain private.

In the beginning of my blogging career, this was so difficult to get my head around because privacy felt like a bit of an alien concept by that point when I was openly talking about the rape and abuse, I experienced when I was younger. Over time, though, I feel that I've pretty much completely mastered the skill of showing respect toward my Mum's opinions of privacy.

The most helpful tool in developing that outlook has been recognising the importance of treating others how you would like to be treat, because, in fairness, there have been times when I've actually said to my Mum "don't tell such and such about that." So, I recognise that the fact there are occasions when I'm comfortable with one person knowing something but not another, illustrate some sort of empathy and understanding with my Mum's thoughts on disclosure.

So, my current stance on this topic in the blogging industry, is mostly centred around the notion of ensuring that the details I discuss online are actually going to be beneficial for myself and/or my readers – in whatever way possible. I find that it gives me motivation and validation to support my decision to give details of some areas in my life which many might define as private or personal. I think helping others can be an important quality where there's a sign that disclosing something might be difficult, overwhelming, or upsetting for me; because it makes that worthwhile and gives it a more selfless purpose – which sometimes holds a greater importance for me.

A Note on The Importance of Trigger Warnings

A perfect lead-on from talking about disclosure is this subject of including trigger warnings – where necessary – in your content because these cautions can most often derive from talking about sensitive, personal matters.

Despite being abused and raped when I was in my teens, I was incredibly lucky to have not experienced a 'flashback' until I ended up in a specialist psychiatric hospital for two and a half years, aged twenty-one. In all honesty, it wasn't even a challenge or difficulty that I'd heard of or witnessed anyone else experiencing until I was an inpatient of the Personality Disorder ward. With statistics showing that most people with a diagnosis of a Personality Disorder have also gone through some sort of trauma or abuse (which is typically the catalyst or trigger to the development and overtaking of the Disorder).

I think that in the more immediate aftermath of the abuse and rape, any flashbacks were likely avoided because I spent the entire Summer after it ended doing all that I could to block it out. I wanted to go beyond forgetting it – I wanted to just erase the entire ordeal even if that left a stain on my life. But my desperation for any sort of relief or loss of memory around it meant that the slightest difference/improvement, would have been more than welcome.

First, I tried using alcohol to cope. Some friends of mine met a group of guys and one of them was older so he had a license and could buy us all drinks! The thing was, where my friends were getting drunk purely for fun, and to have a laugh and enjoy themselves; I was taking it too far. My friends would get really drunk, but then they'd know – and be able to – stop and either make their own way home or sober up and continue having fun. I, on the other hand, would drink and drink and drink, until I blacked out to a point where I didn't know my own name let alone remember what had happened to me.

After a few months of that, the group of friends I had got into a massive fight with another group and when the Police became involved, my Mum really 'encouraged' (chose my words carefully with that one!) me to end those friendships. With those relationships, my coping strategy left too and I felt as though someone had thrown me into a swimming pool at the deep end and before even teaching me how to swim! So, in my desperate paddling to stay afloat and frantic grabbing out for some sort of floating device, I found myself taking hold of my schoolwork.

Due to the nature and details of the abuse and rape I experienced, I had to move to a new School to study for my A Levels. Whilst it was the perfect opportunity to feel as though I was getting a fresh start after all of the chaotic trauma; I was more focused on trying to just survive minute-by-minute than actually using the new school to improve my future! In a way, though, it was the same thing; because my eagerness to keep busy and concentrating on something else meant my grades ended up improving.

When I got to almost halfway through my studying, I found myself tiring and starting to fall behind with my homework and losing a handle on my general understanding of my chosen subjects (Law, History, and Philosophy). It was almost as though I was running out of steam – using up all your attention, time, and effort can be challenging and difficult anyway; but when you're doing it just to stay afloat, it can become even more important and therefore even more exhausting. So, I subsequently began failing my tests and classroom quizzes and assignments etc, and I found myself searching for a new coping strategy because despite it then being over one year since the abuse had ended, it still felt as though it had only happened yesterday!

Almost without putting much thought into it, I found myself restricting my diet in really limiting my food and drink intake and then over-exercising. It felt as though it was the only aspect of my family that I had control over and which I could directly affect and influence. So, when I became underweight, I was advised to see an Eating Disorder Specialist who told me that I matched all but one of the diagnostic criteria for Anorexia Nervosa. When I was bullied, I was called a 'bag of bones' and yet, when I looked in the mirror, all I saw was fat thighs and a big tummy! Ironically, though, now that I weigh a lot more; I'm actually much more confident with the shape and size of my body!

Of course, similarly to my previous attempts to block out the memories of the abuse, the behaviour of restriction and over-exercising was only effective for a short amount of time and when its benefits wore off, I felt panicked and terrified at the thought of how I would cope now. So, obviously in the end, I began hallucinating and – feeling completely hopeless of life getting any better – I made my first suicide attempt.

However, it wasn't until my second suicide attempt and admission to a psychiatric hospital that I finally reported the abuse though. After doing so, I had to go through the extremely difficult and horrendous process of giving a written statement and having a video interview that was so harrowing, debilitating, and devastating that I almost developed the belief: 'they might as well just make me relive it all over again!'

It was so difficult because I hate the thought of discouraging others from reporting their own traumatic experience, but I can't lie and say that it's a piece of cake once you make the decision to do so. I think that the most important thought I kept in the forefront of my mind when I was struggling with this

You're NOT Disordered

monumental process, was that it was worthwhile. I reminded myself time and time again that if me having to answer intruding and detailed questions was going to mean that I'd done all I could to protect others from the same abuse, then it was very much worth it.

For the following three years (2009 – 2012) after reporting the abuse, my records show that I was admitted to hospital on over 60 separate occasions; and that meant my life felt chaotic and rushed. I felt as though I was going from one admission to the next with no real pause or time to think things through in between and therefore I had no actual opportunity to spend any time remembering the abuse nor being mindful of avoiding any potential triggers to memories of it.

Then, in Summer 2012, I made a suicide attempt that led to me being on life support and following that, I was admitted to a specialist psychiatric hospital for the following two and a half years. Within days in there though, the girl who I became closest to, was crying hysterically on the floor in the middle of one of the two corridors on the ward. I remember me and all of the other inpatients being ushered back into our bedrooms and as I went, a member of staff said, "don't worry; she's just having a flashback."

This was the first time I had heard of this word being used in this context and it wasn't until a few weeks later – when the girl and I were having a really deep and meaningful chat – that the concept of a 'flashback' in mental health/trauma was really thoroughly explained to me. Even then though, having no actual, personal experience of this, I struggled to feel understanding and empathy when I would see the other inpatients struggle in this way. Of course, even if you have gone through something the exact same as another person has, there's no guarantee that you could efficiently and effectively know exactly, for certain, how someone else was feeling or the thoughts they were experiencing around it. It's the beauty of mental health — recognising you can try to relate and be empathetic, but you may never feel someone understands you or appreciates what you're going through. Then, it's important to not view that fact as a reason to feel alone and hopeless.

Ironically, just when I was considering the fact that I couldn't relate to any of the inpatients experiencing flashbacks, I had my first one! It happened when we were doing a music concert for the staff and other wards in the hospital when someone began singing this song where literally the entirety of the lyrics is relevant to my thoughts of my abuser, my experience of the abuse, and my feelings around all of that. Prior to hearing it at that time, I hadn't actually made the connection with it before, so I was completely unprepared for the unrelenting distress it almost instantly caused me.

I think that this highlights a massively important reason for including trigger warnings in the content on your blog... I'm one of those people who really enjoys being in control of anything and everything that happens in my life. So, this meant that when I was suddenly back in my abuser's office with him hurting me, I felt totally thrown off-guard with the fact that I had absolutely no warning of that happening. An absence of that prior expectation really contributed to the fact that I pretty much collapsed to the floor, screaming hysterically, gasping for breath, and crying in the most dramatic of ways!

I was genuinely inconsolable; to the point where the hospital staff had to give me a sedative to stop the tears from flowing and to just generally calm down my distress. Nevertheless, I found the fact that you can be going about your day and suddenly reality just disappears and you're back in the worst situation you've ever been in really scary and that took its toll on my mental health. It left me feeling quite hopeless with the thought that no matter how well I was doing or how happy I was feeling, something 'small' could come along and all that positivity and safety was gone – just like that!

Experiencing that flashback also meant a number of other things... Firstly, it meant that I felt a level of empathy and understanding for any other inpatients or mental health service users who go through the same or similar instances.

Having that knowledge and appreciation, then proved really helpful for my blogging career too, because it gave me the necessary experience to be able to feel fairly confident in educating others on the topic via my blog's content. With the notion of helping others in literally whatever way possible being so beneficial and therapeutic for my mental health; developing a whole new knowledge of something really important, was so incredible for me.

Whilst I very obviously wish that I hadn't had to go through what I did to really appreciate the thoughts and feelings of others in this area, I try to hold onto the fact that it has as one of the very few positive results of experiencing flashbacks myself. Plus, having my own instances meant I can really feel confident in the tips and advice I share on my blog because they're genuinely tried and tested coping mechanisms.

So, considering my experiences of flashbacks, and those from others that I witnessed, I feel very certain that providing trigger warnings in a bid to reduce the chance of these occurring, is extremely important. This feels especially true in blogging, because there's such a huge likelihood of it happening with a blog that has the potential to reach an enormous number of people.

An understandable argument to make in discussing the challenges in trigger warnings; would be the fact that it can be incredibly tricky and – in fairness – next to impossible sometimes, to truly recognise absolutely every single triggering statement you might make! This is largely due to the fact that 'triggers' can be so very dependent on an individual and their own, very unique, experiences, relationships, and traumas etc. But this, the fact that a person's 'trigger' can be so completely different to another person, only highlights the importance of including trigger warnings – where appropriate – in your blog's content. If there's a chance that 'only' a handful of people will be affected by a word or sentence you choose to use in a blog post, who will they turn to for support and reassurance that they're not unreasonable for having their specific triggers?

The recognition that psychiatric and mental health support services and helplines etc. can be incredibly inadequate and even inefficient, in providing any sort of positive impact on a person's wellbeing, is an additional reason to be extra cautious in using trigger warnings. Because, if you don't, and your content upsets someone and triggers them to experience a flashback or leads to another difficult consequence, where will they go for help with that?

This, however, then poses the question: how responsible are you for someone's response to your actions or attitude?

I discovered the answer for this towards the end of my two-and-a-half-year long admission to the psychiatric hospital, when another inpatient asked me what I thought it had taken to truly start recovering and to experience this turnaround in my mental stability. I told her that it had been when I had managed to run away from the hospital and make a third suicide attempt that left me on life support. I told her how physically poorly I had felt when I came out of the coma and then the staff then took me to the Psychiatric Intensive Care Unit (PICU) upstairs from the ward I'd been on for over a year.

I explained that feeling so poorly and hopeless and scared was a giant wake-up call to recognise that I didn't want this to be my life. I was exhausted and felt so fed up with living that way – of feeling suicidal and making attempts and being saved. It made me realise that perhaps I just wasn't meant to die; and so – when I was finally allowed back onto the ward from the PICU – I turned my attention to my blog and found myself developing a sense of purpose, determination, dedication, and passion. Feelings which I'd only ever experienced in a negative sense.

Within days of telling this other inpatient what had helped, she was trying to run away, self-harm on the ward, and be generally rude and abusive to the staff. I remember crying and telling the staff and other inpatients that I believed it was my fault she was acting this way. The staff ended up shouting at this girl and saying: "we know you just want to go to the PICU, but there's no way you're going there when you're not genuinely poorly like Aimee was!"

Thankfully, the other girls were supportive of me too and reassured me that this inpatient was a grown adult who was completely in control of her own mind and behaviours. They told me not to feel guilty or to blame in any way because I had only been genuinely answering her question and obviously had no bad intentions or thoughts that she might respond in this way. This experience ended up adding to the staff's almost constant encouragement to take responsibility for your own actions, to accept the consequences, and to cope with them in whatever way you choose to.

With this experience in mind, I actually don't very often post trigger warnings in my content on I'm NOT Disordered because, typically, the titles of my blog posts are extremely explicit as to what the topic is and how in depth I might go in my writing. Where the title doesn't do this, I give trigger warnings and I've never had a problem with someone telling me I should've done it for a post when I haven't. It's all about what's best for your blog and your readers.

You're NOT Disordered

The 2 Greatest Ways to Cope with What You Write

Including trigger warnings in your content is important, but I think that what's even more essential is taking care of your own mental health and general wellbeing when you're writing about potentially upsetting or difficult subjects or experiences. I say that because, at the end of the day, if you're unable to write about them; then there won't be any content to put the trigger warning on!

Being a mental health blogger means that this has definitely been a challenge that I've experienced on a pretty regular basis since creating I'm NOT Disordered in 2013. Initially, this actually wasn't too horrific because my mental health was already so poorly; to the point where I was a sectioned inpatient of a psychiatric hospital when I started blogging. So, it left me in a place where I had the attitude 'it can't get any worse' and that, if it did, at least I was in a safer place than if I were left to my own devices and more able to use my unhealthy coping strategies.

So, to recognise the importance of maintaining your own mental health or wellbeing, here are some tips...

1. Be flexible or have less pressure in your schedule

Every blogger creates their content in a different way/with different apps or computer programmes; so there will be some out there who might find or interpret this part in equally different ways.

So, for me, and the way I blog, I don't often set aside a day or a particular time frame to create content during; mostly because of this tip... I have come to recognise that being flexible in my blogging by not holding myself to some sort of strict and unbudging timetable. For some bloggers, this might not be possible if they have other commitments e.g., a job outside of blogging, or routine appointments etc. So, I'd recommend that even if you do feel that you have no choice in having a content creating regime/schedule, you could remain in a healthier mindset of relieving any really stifling pressure to abide by it.

I think that maintaining some sort of control over what you're blogging about and when you're blogging about it, you'll develop a better sense of comfort or reassurance when you're blogging about difficult topics/subjects/experiences. Personally, I'm very much willing to be branded a 'control freak' because it's an ability and skill that I find really helpful for my mental health. I think that it'd be fair to say a lot of that stems from experiencing hallucinations that have instructed and encouraged me to engage in life-altering coping mechanisms e.g., self-harm or attempting suicide. It meant that I often felt out of control of my own body, mind, and life in general, really.

Being a blogger, has been so helpful to several aspects of my life, and my – almost – craving to be in control; is one of those. With I'm NOT Disordered being such an important aspect of my life, it means that I really like the fact that I'm in charge of what I write and when I write it. It gives me a sense of power and influence to reassure me that my life isn't in the hands of anyone but myself.

Another way pressure can make a difficult and challenging appearance in your blogging/life schedule, is when you feel that you can't fulfil promises you've made to yourself or your readers about something, e.g., if you've said that a blog post will be published on a particular date/time. Doing this, and experiencing a notion of failure with it, can cause more problems and stress for your mental health and for any assumptions you make of how your readers might be feeling. It can be incredibly easy to feel that you're letting people down – especially where you're writing about something difficult and are finding that – in your best interests – you need to take a break from it.

If you're writing about something challenging – whether it's suicide, or animal cruelty in the beauty world, or eating disorders in the fashion industry, or poverty in travel blogging – it can be extremely comforting to allow yourself the time to take a breather. This can work as a bid to ensure that you're not experiencing any undue stress or pressure that might not be necessary.

2. Allow rewarding time for self-care

There's a lot of pressure in the blogging industry and sometimes, you'll see online influencers talking about this publicly and they're often met with a negative, demeaning response. The comeback is usually centred around the idea that those in this industry have opted to be in it and that they have known what they were getting themselves into. Well, having created my blog in 2013 – at a time when there were really only three mental health blogs in the digital world – I can honestly say that out of every single pressure I've come up against; I've expected absolutely none of them! But, now that blogging is much more well known, I can appreciate that anyone who starts creating content more recently might have better insight into what they can expect from it.

In addition to recognising that people who are just starting to engage in this industry will have a better appreciation of the challenges they might face in doing so, it's also important to consider what it means to enter a career like this and then talk about the hardships of it. In all honesty, I think that a lot of the negative thought processes on bloggers who do this, is centred around resentment and often, some sort of jealousy – the grass is always greener on the other side!

With the concern that talking about the drawbacks to this industry online will make you vulnerable to a ton of abuse and trolling; it can be incredibly 'easy' to find yourself internalising the venting you want to do and beginning to struggle from the sheer frustration of feeling silenced and dismissed. It's kind of ironic – the idea that worrying what some readers might think of you being honest and open can render you reluctant to create content and that this then ends up working against your genuinely supportive and interested followers. The thought of – and even just the sheer possibility of – this happening, is something I've found really helpful in spurring me on to continue blogging.

Being somewhat caught 'off-guard' with numerous challenging aspects of blogging meant that I had the distinct notion of learning to walk before I could crawl. This left me feeling quite tired and drained; to the point where I was really in need of some decent self-care in order to find some energy and regain my passion and dedication for blogging. Fortunately, by that point, I had gone through Dialectical Behaviour Therapy (DBT) as treatment for my Personality Disorder diagnosis, and in the Therapy, you're taught about self-soothing and given examples of what this can look like for different people.

Initially, I was very reluctant to voice the self-care activities that I found helpful (taking a shower, doing my hair, doing my nails…) because I was so worried that it would make me appear to be superficial and materialistic. In time though, I recognised that you should be able to talk about these useful things without being judged. I also realised that it was important you do this because it can inspire others to either try these activities or to voice those which they find helpful too.

One key self-care action that is really important and which can apply to bloggers of absolutely any genre and who are writing about any topic – utilise mental health helplines. A common misconception of these sources of help and support is that you need to be suicidal or have a mental health diagnosis to utilise them. This isn't always true. Yes, there are some helplines that are specifically for someone feeling suicidal or who had a particular diagnosis or is/has been in a particular situation; but there are so many other helplines that can provide advice or even just a listening ear. It's also important that you don't consider yourself to be somewhat undeserving of that because you're not struggling to that degree – everyone's mental health is equally important.

"An idea can only become a reality once it is broken down into organised, actionable elements"

Scott Belsky

The Importance of Planning in Blogging

When I first created my blog, I'm NOT Disordered in 2013, whilst I had some really important intentions with it (for it to be therapeutic for myself and to increase the understanding of mental health in my loved ones), I really didn't imagine it would still be going over ten years later. Or that it would have the following it has (over 1.1 million readers at the time of writing this)! This initial absence of believing in my blog's potential and having faith in myself as a Blogger, meant that there was no necessity for any sort of planning or organisation in any part of my blogging.

Viewing your blog as something incredibly casual and lacking in being of some sort of importance or bringing a level of meaning to your life, can really impact how effective planning can be for it. It can alter just how you much you need to engage and develop some sort of planning and organisation techniques that will be ideal for the theme and basic layout or structure etc of your content.

After a year or so things changed, and I started to take my blog a lot more seriously and began deeming it to be a bit of a career. I developed some huge dreams and goals for I'm NOT Disordered and found myself feeling much more confident that it would reach/achieve these. I could see that my blog was helping others and not just myself and with that notion came the realisation that I really needed step it up a notch and feel worthy of the huge influx of readers and all their emails thanking me for various pieces and elements of the content I was creating. So, I began planning...

Something I didn't realise when I first tried to plan my content out was that it can actually take a great length of time to really nail being organised and to actually harness a particular method to do it, in a way that's more affective and more specifically tailored to your content/blog. I thought that planning was planning – there was no real art or skill to it because I thought that everyone benefits from it in the same way. But the thing is, the big (and most important) difference between people who are in need of planning, is that not everyone is doing it for the same reason; and if there are different motivations then there can be different methods with a variety of outcomes. This can mean that even just one person can actually thrive off more than one planning exercise/format.

So, after recognising that I'm NOT Disordered was becoming a whole lot more of a career and a much larger priority with a higher level of importance in my life, I found myself starting to plan my content. Now, personally, I'm a kinaesthetic learner which means that I learn best through the act of doing something. People who excel with this style of learning are often deemed 'avid note-takers' and so I like to plan through using numerous – and I mean numerous! – notebooks. One reason why I actually really love to start a new project is because it means a whole new notebook!

An example of the fact it can take a considerable amount of time to discover, practice, and master planning is that after ten years of blogging, I've finally discovered the brand of notebook I find most helpful in my planning process. I found my first one of the Lola Design company's notebooks in T K Maxx which is a retail store that mostly sells one-off items so when I found the notebook had an ideal layout for me, I couldn't exactly go back to the store and pick up another. So, I ended up scouring the internet for the brand and in almost no time at all, I found myself owning three of their notebooks (which each have amazingly illustrated covers) and having a few more in my Amazon Wishlist!

The element of some of their notebooks I have found so helpful is its layout; every other page has two sections to it which are labelled 'to do' and 'priorities.' The to do section is lined with bullet points, and the part for your priorities is just plain paper. Then, on the other alternate pages, the entirety of it is lined paper and there's a box at the top which is formatted to write the date. I find these really ideal because these are the three most required elements, I need in my planning.

The to do list is ideal for a more general look at almost all the tasks I need to get done throughout the day and it means that if I'm not able to tick everything off by the end of that day, I can easily just add what's left to the next day.

The 'priorities' part is really essential for my planning too as it gives me the opportunity to actually order the most important things, I need to get done that day. It's useful because it encourages you to organise the most time-sensitive tasks too to keep any deadlines. It also means that even if I haven't finished my to do list, I can still feel productive in looking at how many of my priorities are completed – because how satisfying and therapeutic is the act of ticking things off a list?!

The notes page is just as simply useful too because it provides the space to jot things down when you might need to refer to them later in the day – or at a later date completely. I like that this part is lined as well because it means my notes don't look too messy, are more easily located, and are more easily made sense of and translated when I do actually need them!

Before I started using these notebooks and planning my content and projects, I feel that I wasn't truly dedicated or passionate about what I was doing because I wasn't putting a whole lot of thought and time into it. This meant that when I began putting more effort and care into things, I began to feel that I was more deserving of the achievements, the milestones my blog reached, and the incredible opportunities I'm offered through the collaborations I feature and create on I'm NOT Disordered. Finally feeling worthy of the amazing bonuses that were coming from having such a popular and successful blog, was really helpful in building on my confidence in my work in the industry. I felt more and more purposeful in continuing this journey through the digital world and felt fully able and so much more justified in celebrating the accomplishments along the way.

I also found the act of planning massively enjoyable too and I think this is largely because I'm such a huge fan of writing that I'll welcome absolutely and literally any opportunities or moments where I can exercise and indulge in this passion! Thriving and being fascinated by something which, in doing it, can end up benefiting others; is so rewarding and thrilling that it makes sense to me that I would take on anything even remotely associated to it – even if that includes writing to do lists!

Aside from finding the act of planning positive and productive, I think it's also important to recognise that thinking ahead or just thoroughly thinking things through; can also benefit your content or whatever else it is in your blogging career that has caused you to turn to planning. I have definitely found that the content and projects I put more time and effort into through planning, have mostly turned out to be the most popular and the most praised/complimented. This is something that I'm really grateful for because there has been the rare occasion where a piece of content, I feel I've worked really hard on doesn't do too well in terms of its popularity and feedback. In all honesty, I found those instances really difficult to cope with, but I found it really helpful to just focus on how proud I was of the work I'd put into the piece.

6 Rules to Planning & Researching in Blogging

This might sound strange, but I actually think I've done – and learnt – so much more planning and researching with aspects of my blog than I did through my entire education/schooling! I mean, I know I've never really had an academic kind of intelligence – I'm definitely a kinaesthetic learner – and I would much rather do something more creative than reading and studying really deep literature and memorising challenging case studies etc.

Being able to plan and research a lot when it comes to my blog though, has really shown me that it's something I definitely can do, it just seems that the topic I'm looking into really matters to me – to the point where it provides me with the motivation and passion that I need to do these things effectively. If I'm interested in the subject or whatever that I'm putting all of this time into, then I feel more dedicated to planning and researching.

In my years of blogging, I've discovered six basic ways to doing these things (and then I'll tell you about what I think you need to actually be planning and researching) …

1. You need the right format/method e.g., use a notebook or would an online document be better?

2. Google can be your best-friend – it isn't cheating or doing things the 'easy way!'

3. Goodreads.com is the ideal site for finding quotes to add a little 'something' different and relevant to your content

4. Pinterest.com is great for ideas, influence, and inspiration around the aesthetics of your blog and your content including graphics and colour schemes

5. Ensure you're using reputable sites when fact-searching or quoting statistics and case studies etc.

6. Use Canva.com to create brainstorms, vision boards, and other aesthetically pleasing documents relevant to your planning and researching

Why Timing Matters

 When I first created my blog, I'm NOT Disordered and started blogging, I really didn't regard it as momentous at all. I didn't, for one minute, imagine that it would become as important and all-consuming as it has over the ten years of its existence. In my absence of having high intentions and goals for my blog, I generally didn't put a whole lot of thought into the content I produced in the first year or so.

Being a psychiatric hospital inpatient when I first entered this industry meant that I had something to write about almost every single day because there was always something happening – whether that be a drama with other inpatients and staff or me feeling that I was making progress with my mental health. Having so much to blog about meant that I really experienced the notion that I was just naturally creating content without having to put in much consideration or time and effort into it.

This was something, however, that I struggled to be grateful for because on the one hand yes, I wasn't trying too hard to produce the content, but that was only the case because of the situation I was in. I'd very obviously rather not have been in that hospital and struggling to find ways to cope with everything I was experiencing as a result. In time, though, I've gained so much recognition and appreciation for all those early days in my blogging career. As a result of the psychiatric hospital really helping my mental health and steering me into recovery, I became thankful for the admission and that meant I was really appreciative of the content because it really thoroughly documented that incredibly powerful and life-changing journey.

So, it really wasn't until a good six months into I'm NOT Disordered that I really became more conscious of timing and planning in my blog posts. On June 23rd, 2013, I published a piece

I titled an 'Article Review' about a piece that a magazine called Glamour had published regarding rape. I think that the fact my mental health was still fairly poorly (I wasn't discharged from the psychiatric hospital until a year later!), was a huge reason why I actually still wasn't overly worried or anxious at the thought of writing the post that could potentially be viewed as controversial. Plus, one where – if I were to be doing something even remotely similar these days – I would do it all so differently! I would recognise the importance of utilising my planning skills and doing some research to ensure the content was definitely accurate.

From that turning point in my content-producing process/habits, I have found myself becoming so much more cautious and meticulous in creating new posts where the timing of them can really make or break their success and the general response they gain from readers. This tends to be particularly true and useful where it's some sort of Awareness date e.g., Mental Health Awareness Week or World Mental Health Day etc or where the post is concerning a current news story that will lose its relevance should it not be published at the right/best time.

Whilst publishing content at the right time increases the chance of how much attention it will earn, creating content for Awareness dates actually has a big drawback. Marking a particularly important date or a personal anniversary of some sort can leave dedicated, regular readers with the understandable expectation that you will continue to create content on these dates every time they come around. So, it is important that you either prepare for this, or find a way to avoid this happening because ultimately, your blog's content should always be motivated by you otherwise it feels forced and can develop the notion that it's a task do create this content.

How Essential Is It That You Have Control Over Your Blog?

When you're considering the timing and relevance of your content and are planning things out like the date it will be published and a deadline for proof-reading (if that's part of your content-creating process), an element or hint at the subject of control almost always comes into your head. I think that this is partly because in acknowledging your blog post needs to be published at a particular part or on a particular day can leave you with the notion that you're not posting it when you want to. Or it can mean that you're not allowing yourself as much time as you would have liked, to create the content.

With I'm NOT Disordered being a mental health blog, some of the content I create can be difficult and upsetting for me (as well as my readers) and so I can sometimes find myself taking a week or so to put a piece together. Whilst spending so much time on one post is often therapeutic and useful in terms of my mental health around the topic I'm blogging about; I do often wonder whether that length of time is totally necessary. Is it just because I feel that I'm able to take that long? Or do I actually need all of that time?

A lot of the time, my content is fairly deep and honest in a personal way, and I recognise that the subjects I discuss on my blog are more than worthy of time and effort. This leaves me believing that you can't – and really shouldn't – rush a blog post about rape or self-harm (two subjects I've often discussed on my blog). It almost feels insulting or dismissive.

To adhere to this thought process, if there's an abuse anniversary (e.g., November 20th was the start of it and April 20th was the 'end') or a particular Awareness date coming up, I try to begin putting together the content around two or three weeks prior to it. This grants me a whole lot less pressure and stress and avoids the distinct feeling that I'm not putting a whole lot of thought or meaning into it with the worry that it's just a post I need to 'get done.' I'm a firm believer that if content on such difficult topics is done 'wrong' in any way, it can have such a hugely negative impact on its readers and so it's really important that you put your all into it so that you can be filled with the notion that you produced it to the best of your ability.

The one drawback to this (putting your all into your blog content) is that if it doesn't go so well – if it's badly received and shown negative feedback – then you might find yourself struggling to cope because you hold yourself 100% responsible for it. You're almost faced with the fact that there's no one else to blame if the content you've completely controlled the creating and publishing of, is badly received. A benefit to this, however, is the recognition that you can take responsibility for your content and that you aren't having to desperately search for information to figure out who else could take the blame.

It also means, though, that you're in control of the impact it has. You can decide whether there needs to be any element of punishment or what the consequences should look like. This is something I've really benefited from because of the abuse I experienced when I was a teenager. For a long time after it, I felt guilty for the entire thing and blamed myself hugely; thinking that I was deserving of it all. But then, when I eventually reported what had happened, everything went in the opposite direction and when my mental health deteriorated, I found myself taking absolutely no responsibility for my actions and behaviours, and the ways in which they were negatively impacting my family and friends.

Talking about having control over your content though – it isn't just about learning to master deadlines and the timing of your posts – it's also about feeling a sense of pressure or expectation around creating particular content, especially where it's concerning an Awareness date. Having a mental health blog, there are a number of specific dates/week/months dedicated to different illnesses, symptoms, causes etc – so many, that it would be close to impractical and impossible to produce content for every single occasion.

There have been so many occasions where someone (a reader, friend, or anyone really!) has said "what are you going to do for Mental Health Awareness Week?" or "are you not doing content for...?" Sometimes – usually depending upon who it is – these are general, curious and interested questions, but regardless of the intention or motivation, they can come across as stressful and leave you feeling pressured. As though, now that one person has questioned it, it's safe to say that so many others will also be expecting the content; and how do you let all those people down? Especially when you recognise and firmly believe that you and your blog wouldn't be where you are today if it weren't for your readers...?

Gratitude is something I'm extremely passionate about because I really appreciate just how meaningful and important it can be to both the person that is grateful and to those, they are thankful for. I developed this understanding through the abuse and my poor mental health because – when the abuse 'finished', and I entered recovery – I came to recognise that those things might not have happened if it weren't for particular contributing factors (and these factors were sometimes people). Though, admittedly, this mindset – being grateful to those who have saved my life – took a long time to reach. For a good few years, I resented and really hated all the people who were saving me when I truly felt that this was the last thing I wanted. I remember being put on life support after a suicide attempt in 2012 and the last thing I said before I was anaesthetised was "I hope something goes wrong and I die anyway!"

Having my life saved and that doing so, provided me with the opportunity for my mental health to recover and for me to begin blogging; meant I found myself becoming genuinely thankful to those Nurses, Doctors, and all the hospital Security who were having to hold me down until I fell unconscious! I was thankful for the Paramedics and Police Officers who had taken me to the hospital in the first place, and to the Community Mental Health Team who fought for me to be admitted to a psychiatric hospital upon waking from the coma. Mostly, I was – and still am – grateful for my Mum, who has been by my side the entire time.

Showing gratitude and recognising that others (including your readers where you likely don't know every single one of them!) are important and that they matter in your blogging career in particular doesn't have to mean you relinquish control of the content you're creating and publishing. There can be a massive difference between inspiration and influence. The thought of people who are supportive and promotional of your blog doesn't have to mean that you 'owe them one.' It doesn't mean that you need to do what they want and expect because otherwise you'll lose that support and encouragement. But, having felt that way myself, I recognise that it's a challenging thought-provoking difficulty that can come in blogging and where you have incredible readers that hold a huge importance in your life.

Recognising the power, influence, and control that your readers have over your blog and all the opportunities that come from it and the milestones and achievements it reaches, can also bring up a question of recognition. It can leave you debating just how deserving you are of any amazing experiences you have, that are related to your blog in some way. Do you concentrate on the fact that if you weren't creating decent content then you wouldn't have so many readers?

5 Things in Blogging You Should Really Plan & Research

When I first created my blog; I'm NOT Disordered in 2013, I put very little thought into it – I didn't even brainstorm the title; it just came to me! Nor did I consider the pros and cons to blogging; had I done so, I might have originally – and without any experience – listed this aspect (the necessity of planning and researching) in the cons side! Purely because in those very early days I wasn't blogging with any real long-term or serious intentions. I didn't, for one minute, even remotely consider that I would still be doing this and that it would be so massively important in my life.

Because of its importance and meaning for me, I find planning and researching things for my blog actually quite enjoyable and exciting. It feels good to put so much time and effort into making decisions that could really change the way my content is received, the opinions people have of it, and what that means to the opportunities I'm offered as a direct result of my blog's popularity and success. It feels like the ultimate recognition of how much it means to me – it's like saying that I think this is worthy of going the extra mile and doing all that I can to ensure that if I change something or do something new on my blog, I've done so after putting so much thought and consideration into it.

Nothing on I'm NOT Disordered is done on a whim, and this means that if I make a decision after putting so much thought into it, and it seems to turn out to be a mistake, a failure, or a learning curve (depending on how you look at it); I can at least feel confident that I did it with care and thought. So, rather than seeing it as a huge knock to my confidence to think that I've tried really hard and have still been wrong, I look at it as something I've done responsibly and carefully. It means it doesn't become something that I consider feeling regretful about because I didn't do it spontaneously and impulsively.

With my now many years of experience in the blogging industry, I feel that I've definitely learnt the key things in blogging that you really need to be putting extra attention into through planning or/and research...

1. Collaboration pitches and partnership content

If you're about to contact an organisation, brand, company, charity, or well-known person to pitch the idea of working together on content for your blog, it's so important that you put a lot of thought, time, and care into the pitch so that it is intriguing, interesting, and persuasive. Otherwise, it might get you absolutely nowhere and typically, you won't get feedback on what was 'wrong' with your pitch, you'll just be ignored or get a firm and unmoving 'no.'

2. Blog posts on controversial topics

This is something I definitely try to avoid! My thought process in considering to blog about something controversial is to ensure that I feel that expressing my thoughts and opinions on the topic, are worth any rebuttal or spiteful comments I might experience or receive from readers who strongly disagree. If I feel that I can cope with negativity, then I still ensure that the post is fair and shows consideration and understanding to stress that my opinions are informed.

3. Advertorial pieces

If a brand, company, or charity has agreed to work with you/your blog, then your collaboration might often feature 'ads' with you needing to create content that features gifted items or complimentary experiences e.g., hotel stays and train tickets. It's good to spend extra time on these pieces to maintain a sense of being worthy and deserving of these opportunities and to encourage the partner to give you good feedback and to be more likely to work with you again.

4.   Adding pages to your blog

Most blogs have a number of 'pages' to them – with the most commonly named being 'About' or 'Contact.' Making big, fundamental changes like this to your entire blog can be hugely important and can have the potential to impact the popularity of it with some readers finding there to be too many pages, or for it to be difficult to navigate your blog in general. Therefore, it's essential that you do research and planning into how additional pages could change your blog's aesthetic and how this might impact your audience and their opinions of your blog.

5.   A series of blog posts

Creating a series of numerous blog posts that might be on the same topic, or in celebration or recognition of a length Awareness date e.g., Mental Health Awareness Week typically means one blog post a day for the entire Week on I'm NOT Disordered. If you're going to commit to a series of blog posts then it's important that you plan each piece out to ensure there's no repetition, and that you do some research into the best times to publish the content so that it's more likely to be seen by your typical/target audience (if you're going to put a lot of time and effort into a series of content, it's motivational to know that people will actually see it!).

Questions to Ask Yourself Before You Blog

One really important piece of advice in blogging that I would give, is to take the time to think things through, take the time to prepare, and plan things out. When you're deciding whether to disclose some sort of details or experiences, the idea of asking yourself a few questions before you blog can be really helpful in having some sort of motivation to publish it because it can boost your dedication and passion for the post...

In a year's time, will I wish that I hadn't told my readers this?

Is there a risk of instigating controversy with this blog post?

Will anyone else also benefit from this blog post?

Do the possible consequences outweigh any positivity that can come from this blog post?

What will I gain from blogging about this?

"There is immense power when a group of people with similar interests gets together to work towards the same goals"

Idowu Koyenikan

Why I Decided to Feature Collaborations

Having just discussed the importance of putting thought and planning into featuring and pitching collaborations, I thought that led on perfectly to this bit...

When I first created, I'm NOT Disordered in 2013, I had literally absolutely no intention of it becoming all that it is today; and that is especially true regarding all the collaborations I've done over the years. My initial purpose in blogging being to better communicate and explain my thoughts, feelings, and behaviours to my friends and family because I was over 100 miles away in a psychiatric hospital. So, the idea of working with organisations, charities, companies, brands, and well-known individuals wasn't something I even remotely entertained or considered.

Not thinking of doing collaborations, was also affected by the fact that blogging wasn't something that was a 'thing' at that time. So, I struggled to find a real trailblazer who I could look to for guidance and inspiration – someone who could lead the way and set standards to illustrate what bloggers could be capable of doing. After a while though, I found that inspiration in Zoe Sugg aka Zoella, and I watched as she featured in the press, had interviews on TV... and collaborated with huge brands to the point of creating her own range of various products sold in the health and beauty stores, Superdrug and Boots.

By the point of Zoe creating and achieving all of these accomplishments – including reaching 5 million subscribers on her YouTube channel – I'm NOT Disordered was growing in popularity and I was starting to recognise that it was having a massively amazing impact on my mental health. These two things (the popularity and how beneficial it was on my life) felt like huge motivations to follow in Zoe's footsteps and to keep going with my blog. I recognised this meant taking things more seriously and that would mean putting more time, effort, passion, dedication, importance, and care into creating its content.

In looking at Zoe's success and journey, I saw her reactions when she reached another one million subscribers/followers/readers and the joy she exuberantly illustrated in her content was more than enough inspiration to begin working on increasing I'm NOT Disordered's following. Almost consequently – or at least it was a natural result – of doing this, I found myself putting thought into starting to feature collaborative content.

I think that the main reason for this was because I felt the need to be deserving of the popularity and that meant putting more thought and consideration into the standard of the content, I thought I should be creating to meet or qualify for that sense of entitlement. My Mum brought me up with a great work ethic and so I enjoy working hard, attending events, and spending a lot of time on collaborations or other projects because I'm filled with the reassurance that I will have truly earnt any positive and rewarding results to using all that effort and energy.

4 Steps to Decide If Collaborations Are Right for Your Blog

As a Blogger who does frequently publish collaborations or partnership pieces, I feel I can say that as with a lot of aspects in blogging, deciding whether to include collaborations on your blog is something that you really should put a lot of care and thought into. It's so important that you recognise any abilities or limitations to the consequences of making this decision – no matter whether you conclude to feature collaborations on your blog or not because it's such a big change...

1. **Considering your already established readership and/or target audience, do you think they would find collaborations appealing?**

Whilst my initial sole thoughts on who I intended my blog to be for were my friends and family on my private Facebook account; that has definitely – and drastically! – changed over the years. I had originally wanted I'm NOT Disordered to be a source of information for those closest to me with the hope that they'd develop a better understanding of my mental health and everything I was experiencing in the psychiatric hospital I was in over 100 miles away from home.

As time went by though, and word-of-mouth publicity really took hold and saw the size of my blog's audience massively increase to the thousands; I found myself developing new intentions, a wider target audience, and I was thinking up even wilder dreams and goals for my blog! But, when the stats continued to rise and rise and rise, it became – in my opinion – pretty unrealistic to imagine that I knew what all of my readers wanted from my content/blog. And so – particularly since my readers burst through the one million milestone – a lot of my decisions on my content or other elements of the blog, have had to be fundamentally determined by and based upon, my own thoughts and feelings.

Similarly, in relation to collaborations, because I began featuring collaborations fairly early in my blogging career; it meant that I hadn't yet found or recognised the importance of I'm NOT Disordered – not just for me and my mental health, but for my readers too. So, I made the decision based on my own opinions of collaborations and whether I thought I would enjoy working on and producing them.

2. **Do you know how to write pitches, project proposals or press releases? If not, would you be willing to learn?**

You know how people always talk about lying on their CV or other job application documents and forms? That's never something I've done myself, but what I have found helpful when I'm asked whether I know how to do something and I've felt that my honest answer of 'nope' would stand against me in getting the job; I usually just say that I don't know, but that I'm a fast learner and I really enjoy learning new things. These things aren't lies, but they are a more productive and positive spin on the fact I can't do something I might need to do in the new job.

The useful aspect of this scenario is that there'll be people in the organisation who can teach me how to do something I have no clue about. In the blogging industry however, whilst I look to other bloggers as inspirational and influential rather than with competitiveness and jealousy; if I want to try something new on, I'm NOT Disordered, I tend not to approach other bloggers to ask for advice and tips on doing it. I think that my need for independence in this respect of blogging, is largely because I like to be responsible for everything on, I'm NOT Disordered. Although, I'm definitely not shy about using Google to find 'how-to...' guides!

It's kind of ironic and kind of like a full circle, to be honest. When I first started blogging, I had no real knowledge of computers and websites, and I ended up having another inpatient do the design work for me. But, this meant that when the Doctors were discussing her discharge before my own, I recognised I needed to figure things out for myself because I couldn't keep contacting her at home every time I wanted to make a design change or something. Think that learning how to do things for myself, has been a great move in my blogging career; and so I wasn't at all reluctant or intimidated to learn when it came to writing pitches etc.

3. Are you a team player? Would you be willing and able to share content control with others?

It actually wasn't until I got my first voluntary job in the Marketing and Communications world, that I really recognised that I had been working alone in my blogging career. This recognition came when with the fact that I found myself having to ask others for permission to do things or to check over my work before it could be printed or published online etc. It was a strange and unfamiliar notion to me, and whilst I completely understand the need to have that process and a hierarchy in the workplace, I did initially struggle with the entire concept because I was so used to having 100% control over things.

I think that it was really through this volunteer role that I began to raise my game in the blogging industry and crank my collaborations up a notch! It not only taught me how to go about working as a team, but also, how important it can be to do that – how it can significantly increase the chance of the work you produce being of a higher, more popular, and successful quality.

I found this out in realising that everyone has their own job title and responsibilities in the workplace because everyone has their own strengths and passions. Learning this meant that I found myself being more aware of exactly what my content was regarding in making better judgments as to whether I really was the best person to speak about those subjects. In some cases, this meant recognising that to enhance the quality of a blog post, it would be helpful to produce it in collaboration with someone or some organisation that was more knowledgeable, better experienced, and therefore more accustomed to talking about the subject.

The real difficulty I had here, was adjusting the realisation that I wasn't the only person in control of the content... I could put collaboration pieces together but then the partner would be able to dictate any edits. In all honesty, my confidence was pretty low when I first started collaborating with others because it was usually a case of me approaching them with the worry that I didn't have enough readers to be seriously considered as worthy of others working alongside me and putting their name to my blog. This lack of confidence meant that I would often publish content I wasn't 100% happy with, but which the partner was.

I worried it would be arrogant if I turned around and spoke up and feared the collaboration would disappear and go against my reputation when pitching to others. As the readership grew though, and organisations started approaching me, I found myself feeling a bit more entitled to put my foot down where I didn't agree with edits others made. Having gone from the lower, more conscious state to recognising I have some sort of influence; has meant that I have so much gratitude and consider myself so lucky to be able to have this new stance.

Recognising that I might not be in that position if it weren't for my readers though, has added to my determination to only publish content that I believe they would be happy with too.

You're NOT Disordered

4. What do your initial thoughts and instincts tell you to do here?

I'm someone who definitely believes in listening to your gut and believing in your instincts – particularly with my blog, and actually, also with the health of my pets and myself! But, with my blog; I'm NOT Disordered, I feel like all of the best things that have happened with it are things that came about without any real planning or preparation – even the most fundamental aspects of it like creating it and naming it!

On January 6th, 2013, I had a really productive and helpful 1:1 with my Key Nurse in the psychiatric hospital I'd been an inpatient in for almost one year. In it, I agreed to begin writing letters for the staff detailing instances linked to the abuse I had experienced in a bid to put the staff in a better position in providing me with more effective and efficient help and support. From the time it took to leave that meeting room and walk down the corridor to my bedroom I had made the decision to make some sort of record of things because it felt like I was finally taking a step onto the road to recovery.

Then, walking into the room and seeing my laptop sat on the bed? I knew – without doing any research or ever even having previously entertained the idea - I knew I was going to start a blog! In keeping with everything that had already occurred (or not occurred depending on how you look at it), I just went and created an account on Blogger without weighing up other platforms, and I typed in 'I'm NOT Disordered' without even so much as a brainstorm!

So – from the offset – I've trusted my instincts with decisions surrounding my blog, though as the readership has built to – what feels to me like – dizzying heights; I've found myself putting more thought and consideration into instances where I need to make a decision that could have a large impact on either/both myself and my life outside of blogging, and/or on my blog's readers. I think this has become the case because I have more appreciation and recognition of how much my blog decisions matter to a larger number of people than just me! But I still always keep in mind what my gut feeling is and weigh up how practical that is and what could reasonably result from it.

"Disappointment is real, but do not get discouraged"

Lailah Gifty Akita

The 2 Main Reasons for A 'No' To Collaboration Pitches

I won't lie, it isn't often that I've received a negative response as a refusal or reluctance to collaborate when I've pitched an idea of a partnership to an individual, organisation, brand, charity, or company etc. Especially recently. But I think that one of the largest reasons why this has changed, has been that I've learnt a lot about how to write an effective, positive, meaningful, persuasive, and encouraging collaboration pitch. I have, however, received enough negative responses to be experienced and knowledgeable enough to write this section!

1. Your statistics

I'll never forget when I was celebrating a reader's milestone not long after starting to blog, and another blogger turned around and asked why I cared so much about 'the numbers.' I was completely taken aback because I was so completely used to everyone being supportive and joining me in the excitable screaming. I had not only never been asked this, but I'd also never thought about or considered it myself, so that meant I had no real, well-thought-out answer.

Now though, I've had over ten years to think about it(!) and to arrive at a really effective and genuine answer... So, firstly, I think that my most favourite aspect of having a huge audience, is that it means I have a greater chance of being able to help someone. In all honesty, as therapeutic as I find blogging and writing about my thoughts, feelings, and experiences; I might not be as open and honest as I am if I didn't have the genuine hope that doing so, might help another person. In fact, I don't know where my blog, I'm NOT Disordered, would be if it weren't for its readers. I mean, how would I have gained all the opportunities that I have?

That, the recognition and acceptance that my readership has played a huge – and almost essential part – in the collaborations I've secured, comes from the realisation that when I didn't mention my blog's statistics in my collaboration pitches, I pretty much almost consistently got absolutely nowhere with them! I think a huge reason why I wasn't talking about the number of readers was because the girl who'd questioned my reasoning for finding them important had left me questioning just how genuinely invested it meant that I was in I'm NOT Disordered. I worried that talking about the number of readers made me appear superficial and as though my priorities are misplaced. As though I'm only blogging for the attention and the social status and reputation that come with being able to say you have a popular blog or a particular number of readers.

In viewing readers as opportunities to help someone else, I became more and more confident and willing to begin featuring my blog's statistics in my collaboration pitches. Doing so and seeing that the chance of a positive response to the pitch was massively heightened by mentioning the reader count and other statistics, meant that I began to learn why these things also mattered to those I was wanting to collaborate with.

I realised that in approaching a prospective partner, there really needed to be something beneficial in the collaboration for them too. I mean, why would they commit whatever you're asking for – whether that's their time, their money and other resources, or even just their name and reputation, if they stood to gain nothing by it? It's about putting yourself in their shoes too and considering why you would want to benefit from something you had to commit to, or which required you to invest something in.

There might be some out there who would argue that this is selfish and that you should do something good because it's good and because you want to. Like doing a 'good deed' – you shouldn't do it just to get a thank you or to look good doing it...

But let's be real and let's recognise that the blogging industry is an incredibly fierce and competitive area to work in, and if you want to keep working in it, you need to have a degree of fierceness in yourself. A level of convincing confidence that sells. The only great problem I've experienced here though, is where you're so very proud and happy with your audience size, yet it still isn't 'good enough' for the prospective collaboration partner. This can be really defeating and disheartening, but it's important to remember that this isn't personal - it's not about you being inadequate or your readers being unimportant. It's typically and genuinely just a business decision.

2. The idea

I think that one of the most obvious reasons to decline a collaboration pitch is the belief that the actual, fundamental idea behind it isn't quite right. Typically, this will be the case where you haven't completed any research before pitching the collaboration and it's meant you've put forward an idea that they've actually already either tried and failed, or tried and just don't want to repeat themselves. The irony here, though, is that even if they had been willing to try it again, they might be unsure to do it with you if your failure to have already known this looks as though you've not put a lot of time and thought into your pitch. And that? That can say a lot of terrible things about you. It could look as though you're requesting the collaboration for the wrong reasons e.g., a freebie or complimentary opportunity, or that you're not actually dedicated or passionate to work with a particular organisation – you'd work with anyone who says 'yes!'

If the idea hasn't been repetitive, there are several other reasons why it might not be quite right for the organisation you've pitched it to... Here's the top 5:

1. It's not a cause or topic they support
2. It's too risky in terms of it becoming controversial

3. The workload they already have on
4. It's not in continuity with their current work
5. It's irrelevant for their own target audience

To avoid this, it's obviously worth doing as much research as possible to give you a better chance of pitching something they will agree to. However, there's always the chance that you have an idea to pitch that's a bit different to the usual work of the organisation, but which you think will work really well for you both. In that instance, it's incredibly important that – in the pitch – you include your rationale for this belief or opinion.

Many organisations or bloggers are sceptical about trying out new things when they've built a huge following doing things the way that they do, so it's essential that you include information that will convince them to recognise the positive outcomes that might come from doing something different. In managing to successfully persuade others to try your new idea, you'll likely gain a more productive, memorable, reputation than someone who pitches something very similar and unoriginal. In contrast to the hesitant ones, there are still so many marketing and communications departments/teams who recognise just how refreshing it can be to have a 'fresh pair of eyes' who can come up with more creative and unique ideas. It would actually be a really clever idea to include in your research which mindset the organisation you're pitching to, tend to have and utilising that knowledge and insight in your pitch.

The Most Powerful Response to Rejection

In the world these days, there's a lot of talk about revenge and having a really enviable and phenomenal comeback when someone does something terrible to you – particularly online. There are countless opportunities for people to be spiteful to one another in the digital world and being a blogger and talking about your life, can really open you up to that and increase the chance of you experiencing any horrible comments/messages.

Whilst, in my entire blogging career (over ten years) I've only experienced a total of three horrible comments on my blog; I'm NOT Disordered; I don't think there's been a single day where I've logged into social media and not seen at least one hateful post about some topic, trend, or person – or all three! However, I do believe that receiving a nasty or jealous message from some horrible account managed by someone who has a handful of followers and is basically hiding behind the anonymity of their keyboard, is a whole different ballgame than a full organisation saying they don't want to work with you (no matter what the reason).

It might be surprising considering that my blog now has over one million readers, but believe me; there were a few instances where my pitches to collaborate with a few brands and one charity were rejected and I was a given a big, fat, disappointing, 'no.' These were, of course, in the beginning of my blogging career when I'm NOT Disordered wasn't really established and I put little to no serious thought into the pitches. In them, I would just talk about how much a collaboration would mean to me... I wouldn't present my statistics, I didn't discuss how they would benefit too, I didn't include what I would like their role to be in the collaboration.

I think that my lack of thought, dedication, passion, and consideration in my pitches was largely born from the fact I lacked all of those thoughts and feelings around blogging anyway. I hadn't yet formed the incredibly massive and important affinity I now have for my blog and the communications and marketing industry on a whole. Thankfully, in developing those thoughts, feelings, and opinions of this world, I also found the answer to the question: "what's the most powerful response to rejection?"

Success!

In the beginning of 2023, I began looking for a voluntary job, and after a few interviews, I received a couple of negative responses which detailed that I hadn't been successful for the role, but that the organisation would really like to work with me as a blogger and use I'm NOT Disordered as a publicity opportunity. At the time of those emails, I felt my confidence shred slightly and found myself completely 'agreeing' to both their reasoning for not adding me to their team and the request to feature on my blog.

Then I landed my role as Head of Marketing and Communications for Time To Inspire – a new company offering help, support, and guidance for parents going through legal difficulties and mental health problems – and the irony was that all those negative decisions? Well, they were all regarding roles I didn't want even half as much as this one and they were all roles with a much lesser place in terms of their hierarchy in the industry. So, once my position was completely confirmed all the subsequent tasks and obligations were finished, I found a huge surge in my confidence and ended up developing the strength and motivation to email those other organisations and tell them that 'due to my recent appointment as Head of Marketing and Communications, I will be unable to commit to the time it might take to put together content promoting your organisations.' Boy, did that feel good?! It felt like a professional way of saying; "turns out I'm better and worth more than what you led me to believe I was!"

This feeling and experience was a huge reminder of the early days in my blogging career when so many people were confident that it wouldn't amount to much and that I wouldn't even maintain it for that long. Having started I'm NOT Disordered as a sectioned psychiatric hospital inpatient, when I talked about creating it with the Occupational Therapists and Activity Coordinators, and they asked why it would be any different that other projects I've began. They explained their belief that they felt I would become passionate and eager about a particular industry or job or project, and before completing it or even getting very far with it, I would find some excuse to quit or change my mind.

I recognised that they named this belief as an 'observation' in a bid to make me feel a lack of motivation or reason to question them. To leave me feeling as though it would be pointless to doubt them or argue the point because they had 'seen' it. That insinuated that there were real examples and evidence to support their theory.

Every single time I reach a birthday or reader milestone on I'm NOT Disordered; I really hope that those staff are still reading it! I hope they see me still blogging over ten years later. I hope they know that it now has over one million readers. Believe me, it's difficult to recognise that even ten years later, their words still echo around my head, and I still think of them; but I'm so grateful that I'm thinking about them because they were so incredibly wrong!

You're NOT Disordered

"Celebrate when it's time to celebrate but work hard before you even think about celebrating"

Anuj Jasani

Reasons to Celebrate in The Blogging Industry

The fact that I had previously never really been one to blow my own trumpet in life, to talk about my achievements, nor to acknowledge my skills and talents; actually, had a bit of a negative impact on my blog and its success and popularity in the first year or so. I honestly believe that in the blogging industry and the digital world in general, self-promotion can be a hugely essential key to increasing the awareness of yourself, your blog and/or your social media accounts. Then, in building on that publicity, so many other opportunities can come into play that could bring a huge sense of achievement...

Statistics Milestones

When I was still in the psychiatric hospital where I began my blog; I'm NOT Disordered, another inpatient who also had a blog asked me why I held so much importance to reaching reader milestones. Knowing her, it hadn't been a genuine, curious question; it was a dig and a slight hint toward the notion that doing so makes me superficial or questions my motives in blogging altogether.

At the time, that was upsetting and embarrassing, but now it's much later, I'm glad she asked me because it gave me a nudge to recognise that she might not be the only person thinking this about me/my blog and in asking me, it provided me with the opportunity to begin thoroughly thinking through my answer in case I was asked again. I came to the conclusion that there were two reasons why I hold so much importance to achievements in the statistics:

Firstly, I'm incredibly aware that each 'number' on my reader count (permanently located on the left side of my blog) represents a person! An individual who has found out or been told about I'm NOT Disordered and who has felt encouraged to actually take a look at my content. For me, attracting readers largely translates to an increase in the opportunity for my content to help others in some way.

Now, with me finding blogging to be so therapeutic for my mental health, it means that from the very first emails and comments I received telling me that my content had helped someone else, I felt that I could truly appreciate and understand everything that meant. I was capable of recognising how important it is to find something helpful for your mental health; something that improves your safety levels and can bring a more stable and healthy balance to your life, and, what's even more important, actually having the ability to recognise what it is that's helping you. I can also understand how majorly special it can be to have the insight, courage, and the appreciation to be able to tell someone else that they've been helpful for you. So, these emails, comments, and the shares or direct messages on social media telling me that someone has benefited from something I've written, hold an enormous amount of importance for me.

The second reason why I like to celebrate statistics milestones – and why that tends to be particularly the reader count – is because I completely recognise that my blog wouldn't be what it is today without its readers. I mean, the fact it helps me would obviously give it a good chance that I would still be blogging all these years later; but I can't imagine that I'm NOT Disordered would have the reputation that it does in the industry. I mean, no one would have heard of it and that would very clearly leave there to be absolutely no reason for it to be listed as the number one blog about Borderline Personality Disorder in the entire UK!

When I first decided that I wanted to feature collaborations and partnership content on my blog, I would write pitches and I almost immediately found out that if I didn't mention the size of, I'm NOT Disordered's audience then I would typically get a negative response – or no response at all! Yet, in mentioning how many new readers my blog gets per day and the all-time reader count; I almost always received a very eager and excited 'yes!'

In all honesty – and I don't want to or mean to sound ungrateful here – I sometimes struggled with this recognition that talking about the size of my audience convinced brands and charities and individuals to work with me because it led me to question whether that meant that neither myself, nor my blog on its own; were enough of an asset or attraction to make others interested in collaborating. However, as with many elements of blogging, over the years of my career in this industry, I've learnt a lot about this. I eventually recognised that even though chances are not everyone who reads I'm NOT Disordered will like the content; it wouldn't have all these readers it does if the content I create and publish was absolutely terrible and completely useless! So, there must be some degree of positivity there?!

In addition to feeling that pride and sense of achievement in celebrating my all-time statistics for my readers, I also recognise the importance of your blog's statistics and I actually frequently use the daily reader count to shape my content... I utilise these figures in my content creation by using them as a good illustration of which type of content is most popular and which days of the week and times of the day are the occasions most of my readers typically tend to be online. Ironically, having this research-based insight, can be used to end up having a hugely beneficial impact on that reader count going up even further!

Landing A Collaboration

In the early years of I'm NOT Disordered – when I first decided to begin featuring collaborations – there were only three well-known mental health blogs at that time. One by a Police Officer who had an interest in mental health law, one by a Psychiatric Nurse, and one by someone who had once been admitted to a psychiatric hospital. There were no well-known blogs written by a current inpatient – as I was then – so that meant there wasn't so much... competition – I suppose – is the right word... I hesitate there because I like to think of other bloggers as inspirational and influential rather than viewing them with jealousy. But I think that seeing them as 'competition' can be a healthy balance here – it can instil a healthy sense of drive and determination to better your blog and to strive to bigger and better goals.

This lack of other similar blogs/bloggers meant that when I decided that I wanted to start featuring collaborations on I'm NOT Disordered, I wasn't faced with too huge a challenge because I had accidentally – and very luckily! – stumbled upon a niche. My blog was of a whole new category and totally original in the mental-health-blog industry, so how could any prospective collaborator turn my pitch down? Where else would they turn to?

Another component to the ease of landing collaborations in the beginning of my blogging career, was that 'blogging' really wasn't so much of a 'thing.' It wasn't even really an industry – and it certainly wasn't a trend and those who 'worked' in it were not a popular topic/subject of conversation. I think that in 2013, the most popular use of the internet and social media in particular, had actually just converted from MySpace to Facebook! I honestly think too, that I can put a finger on the exact moment I noticed blogging actually taking off – it was when Zoe Sugg or 'Zoella' (as her blog and later, her brand, was known as) began reaching millions of readers and featuring on TV and in multiple magazines.

In confirmation of this, Zoe gave an interview on Loose Women – a popular chat show with a panel of women in the UK on the TV channel ITV – in June 2014 and afterwards, in her 'vlog' on YouTube, she talked about how she felt as though she'd been a bit of a trailblazer and representative of everyone in the whole blogging/vlogging industry. She also talked about how she hoped she had made everyone proud and had done justice to this area of the digital world.

So, with the start of this publicity of blogging being just one year after I created I'm NOT Disordered, it seemed as though I had not only nailed things in terms of the niche, but, I'd also nailed my timing in it allowing me to be able to have a year to really harness some skills and figure a few challenges out to learn a lot – particularly about collaborations – before my blog became more popular and its reputation took on a more important quality. Ironically, it meant that for all the partnerships I worked on in that time when my blog was almost the only choice in wanting to collaborate with a blogger who wrote from the perspective that I held; resulted in the fact that myself – and my blog – had a huge amount of experience and became more renown for the years when mental health blogs began to spring up all over the internet! So that even when there were more options – or competitors – I'm NOT Disordered maintained its standing in terms of popularity and, if anything, continued to grow and develop into earning thousands of readers a day and this meant it began to gather media attention.

Over the more recent years, I've found that I've gained a much larger amount of confidence around my blog career and that's meant I've found myself striving to go bigger and better in terms of collaborations and other projects/series of blog posts such as 'Blogmas' (when I produce daily, festive content from December

1st to the 25th)! So even though when I first began to put these festive series' together, I did already do so with an element of partnership because I had various – from a Teacher on a Channel 4 series to a Police Inspector! – people complete the same Christmassy Q&A. That first series was in 2015 so I'd had two years of blogging and felt I'd built up a directory of incredibly powerful and well-known contacts, and I had experienced the recognition that people can actually be incredibly curious about the lives of others – particularly, others who they might not know and who they may never meet.

Now, for some reason – which I don't at all recall! – I didn't create a Blogmas series the following year, but I do recall missing having that purpose and demand of effort and time that I could express in a perhaps more creative way than a typical blog post would enable me to. I also really missed the opportunity to really make the most of the festive period and properly celebrate and be engrossed in everything it means and entails. That recognition for the missed opportunity meant that in December 2017, I created a new, festive Q&A, branded the series as 'the 12 Days of Christmas with I'm NOT Disordered' and again, I reached out to those I'd come to know and work with over the years to answer the questions that ranged from 'do you have any funny Christmas memories/stories?' to 'what are your favourite Christmas movies?'

In contrast to the 2015 Blogmas, in 2017 I'd built up a greater figure of readers than I had ever expected or could have ever dreamed about, and so – on multiple occasions – I'd experienced the benefits of having such a large following. So, with the hope of earning more one-off opportunities and long-term partnerships, I had discovered and accepted that working with others would increase the popularity of my blog because it meant my blog would then also gain the following of those who were being featured.

In Christmas of 2018, the notion that collaborations really worked in my blog's favour, and with its popularity now seeming to be steadily on the rise all the time, I felt I could have a bit more 'fun' with the series and so I named it 'the 12 Cats of Christmas' and so it was created and published in partnership with the UK's largest feline welfare charity: Cats Protection. I thoroughly enjoyed zoning in the series on one organisation/one theme and I loved how different and unexpected it was because there is obviously so much digital content out there at Christmas time that it can be extra challenging to be original, unique, and to think of content that will stand out from the crowd.

So, I used that thought process creating the Blogmas series in 2019 when I decided to start actually doing a blog post every single day of December (rather than the 12 days as the previous were) and to turn the entire series into a bit of a competition by working with a few different Etsy stores. I bought items from each store and was then gifted an additional one to put in the competition prize. In hindsight, it was kind of stressful because I had never run a competition before on, I'm NOT Disordered, and I wrongly just assumed (something you should generally never do in blogging anyway!) it would be straight-forward. That learning curve meant that for Blogmas of 2020, I simply chose a theme for the entirety of the twenty-five posts: recommendations.

The simplicity of this and the fact that this meant the posts were so much less stressful and time-consuming to put together, actually made things a bit more enjoyable too! Which meant that for 2021, I decided to trial doing a mixture of my favourite elements from the previous series' by choosing a theme (budgeting) and collaborating with one company; Pretty Perfect Products – who had designed a Christmas Planner that seemed so well-suited for the chosen topic/theme – and which meant the series was dubbed; Budget Blogmas! Again, landing the collaboration was massively motivating and a lovely moment that I cherished so much that I decided the following year – 2022 – to instead, secure several different collaborations with a whole variety of organisations, companies, charities, brands, and stores, etc.

Blogmas this year (2023) though? Well, that will top them all!

Feedback

A number of years ago – in 2017 – I created and published a blog post titled: 'You CAN Get Through Reporting Your Trauma,' and shortly afterwards, I received an email that I have never forgotten and which – when I talk about it and tell someone about it – I still experience goosebumps!

It was from an older lady who told me that she had suffered sexual abuse by a family member when she had been a child and that she had never spoken about it before nor reported it to the Police. After reading that blog post though, she said she'd finally felt reassured that it was the most right, manageable, and brave step to take. This helped her to find the confidence in her capability to remain strong and safe in calling the Police and going through the entire process of reporting the abuse (which actually included a number of instances of rape too).

As though, hearing she had been so courageous as a result of my little blog post wasn't a proud and huge enough piece of news; the email got even better! It turned out that the Police arrested the family member and though I don't know the details in terms of whether he admitted to it, or witnesses were called or there was a trial or anything, the lady told me he actually ended up being sentenced to a number of years in prison.

Now, how incredible is that? Because – when you think about it – that means that a criminal/predator has been taken off the street/out of the public community. Then, this could very likely mean that the lady's actions in reporting everything, could have saved so many more people from being abused by this person (because if an abuser doesn't face any consequences, what reason would they have to not repeat their criminal behaviours?).

Whilst I give so much credit to that brave lady, I also still recognise – as she enforced a number of times in the email – the role that I/I'm NOT Disordered played in this incredible instance! It actually results in a sort of similar notion that I get when I even so much as remotely think about the very real fact that over one million people are reading what I write and viewing the content I produce – it gives me, like stage fright! I 100% recognise that if I allowed myself to actually focus on this and really keep it in my mind, I likely wouldn't be able to type/create anything – I'd be far too stunned and intimidated... Stage fright.

Another instance of positive feedback which wasn't through my blog, but which has gone on to influence the content I create and everything I mentally and physically put into that content; came from a training session with my local Police Force. I teamed up with staff from my local NHS mental health Trust; Cumbria, Northumberland, Tyne, and Wear NHS Foundation Trust (CNTW) and the Mental Health Lead for my local Police to facilitate mental health training for one of their massive intakes of new recruits. In the training sessions, the recruits were taught about their legal powers under the 1983 Mental Health Act and were given scenarios of various versions of a mental health crisis to test and check their knowledge, understanding, responses, and reactions. Then, at the end of the session, I gave a little talk about my experiences in interactions with the Police during a lot of my own mental health crisis instances and there was this one occasion in particular that I would talk about.

I was detained under Section 136 of the Mental Health Act and sat with a female Police Officer in a room in the A&E of one of my local hospitals when I began hallucinating a rabbit. The Officer noticed that I was staring at a completely empty space under a plastic chair on the opposite side of the room and she asked what I could see, I told her and before I knew it, she lifted the chair and stamped her boot all over the space until I told her the rabbit had gone. I had never felt so validated, comforted, and reassured, and those notions meant that I was so much more co-operative with the Police and then the other professionals when I was sectioned at the assessment from the 136.

A little while after one particular training session, one of the new recruits actually got in touch with me via Facebook and said that she'd really listened to everything I had said and that she'd been out to a mental health crisis that day. She told me that all the Officers there felt they couldn't get 'through' to the person in the crisis who was hallucinating a 'devil' and so, this new recruit – remembering my example with the rabbit – ended up chasing this 'devil' around the kitchen before finally flushing it down the sink! The recruit told me that the woman had benefited so much from that feeling of being believed that she engaged and cooperated with the rest of the process in the Police taking her to a psychiatric hospital for an assessment to be admitted.

I felt slightly stunned that my little five-minute talk had gone on to have such a big, important impact and it really lent itself to my blogging because previously, I hadn't really registered the prospect that professionals were reading it! So, I began putting more thought into how I could blog about my own experiences, my thoughts, my feelings, and my actions, in a way that would advise professionals on how best to help and support someone else who might also feel that way, have similar thoughts and experiences, and/or use the same coping strategies etc.

Receiving positive feedback is very obviously a reason to celebrate, but negative thoughts and comments on the content you've created and your blog in its entirety, are equally important. Rather than seeing them as a criticism and a means to pick apart your confidence, undermine all your hard work and all your content decisions; they really should be viewed as learning curves, challenging lessons, and opportunities to make changes and improvements. In fairness – although you can't exactly make a toast about them, these more negative comments can actually result in being a whole lot more productive than an entire ton of compliments!

Anniversaries

I'm such a huge fan of marking anniversaries and I love creating content for these celebratory moments that – for me – have varied from recognising how long I've had one of my pets, to another year of being in my own home since the two-and-a-half year admission to the psychiatric hospital, to talking about the changes I've made through another week under the care/on the caseload of my local NHS Crisis Team.

In life – but particularly, in mental health – things can change so quickly and, often, it can almost seem like you've blinked, and everything is different. It's ironic because in a recent mental health relapse, my antipsychotic medication was increased and upon warning me that it could take up to one to three weeks to experience any benefit; I voiced that was great but that for me – being the one who's actually struggling – that felt like forever away and I honestly couldn't envision myself making it that far safety wise. However, now it's almost three weeks and the increase started working around a week or so ago it feels like not a huge amount of time had to pass to make this happen! It's also felt as though my thirty-five days (as it will be on my planned discharge meeting) under the Crisis Team's caseload have gone fast too!

I feel that this is something that can happen with a lot of anniversaries though – they either feel like they've crept up on you really slowly or that the time has just whizzed by! This – time whizzing by – is what I'd say applies to the one anniversary that I have marked/celebrated every single year of the ten years I have been blogging for – I'm NOT Disordered's Birthday/the date I created my blog (January 6th).

I've found it so rewarding, overwhelming, and proud when I've sat down and taken the opportunity to look through everything that's gone on with my blog in the past year. It's incredible to see its popularity rise, to see me doing more and more one-off opportunities, to see my collaborations grown and develop, and to be given more senior roles and a lot more of responsibilities in events etc.

I think that the pleasure from celebrating the anniversary of my blog's creation comes mostly from the fact that when I first started blogging, I really had no huge expectations from it. I didn't for one minute imagine that it would be all that it is today! I wasn't the only person either – of course my loved ones supported me doing it; but no one was really of the impression that it would still be going ten years later nor that it would be and mean all that it does today. So, making it this far is almost like proving people wrong or just proving – to myself and others – that I'm capable of doing something this big, important, and special.

3 Steps to Staying Humble & Grounded

Now, I'm never really one for blowing my own trumpet, but I recognise that if you want your blog's popularity to increase then you're going to need to do a bit of self-publicity. Word-of-mouth can, in my opinion, be the greatest publicity you can get because people are more trusting of those they know, rather than an advert they see on TV etc. So, it means that it's almost essential that if you want your blog to be popular and to raise awareness of its existence, you have to either have the confidence – or be able to fake it, at least! – to talk about your blog amongst complete strangers!

In fairness, I think that it has taken me years to finally be more confident and comfortable talking about my blog and telling people about its achievements, collaboration history (name-dropping!), other opportunities secured, and accomplishments. The way I've found this confidence has been in recognising that I want my blog; I'm NOT Disordered, to help others and to do this, I need to spread the word about its existence. Finding that motivation has been the key.

In achieving and celebrating milestones and special moments in your blogging career, I think that one of the hardest challenges on you as a person, can be in remaining grounded and humble. I would willingly admit to struggling with maintaining this quality – I mean, how can you not when you're talking about the fact you have over 1 million people reading the blog you've put so much time and effort into?! How can that pride and sense of achievement not encourage you to feel on top of the world? The important thing is not to feel that you're in any way 'above' or 'better than' others – especially when it comes to the size of your audience. It's a massive achievement, but it shouldn't impact your opinion of others – just yourself.

In addition to being humble and grounded being nice qualities in general, and helpful and encouraging for relationships with loved ones, they're also things that can be channelled and illustrated through your content too and can result in it becoming more appealing. I think that audiences – particularly of mental health blogs – tend to gravitate and benefit most from content that is written, created, and published by someone who has good qualities about them as a person and not just their talents and skills in their content creation.

So, with all of this in mind, here are three steps that can help you to stay humble and grounded no matter how big the blogging achievement or how incredible the celebration of them...

1. Always remember your beginning

There's this saying or a quote about how tall trees grow from small acorns, and I always think about it when I consider the beginning of, I'm NOT Disordered and the start of my blogging career as a whole. I feel like it's kind of an accurate summary of how my blog came to be all that it is because it was born from the smallest of ideas/inspirations – and now look at it!

In 2013 on January 6th, after being in the psychiatric hospital for around six months, I had a 1:1 with my Key Nurse and found myself agreeing to begin writing about the abuse I had experienced when I was younger, and which was believed to be the catalyst for my mental health deterioration for the staff to read. My Key Nurse – and I agreed with her – thought it would be helpful for them to help and support me more effectively if they knew more about what I'd been through.

Agreeing to write about this hugely life-changing traumatic experience for people who were arguably really still complete strangers, after taking two years to even finally report it to the

Police, felt like a massive step forward into my recovery journey. As I walked the short distance down the corridor on the ward from the meeting room, we'd had the 1:1 in my bedroom at the far end, I felt a plan forming. Or an idea. Without putting much thought into it at all, I decided I wanted to document my recovery journey and when I got to my bedroom to see my laptop sat on my bed as though waiting for the momentous occasion; it felt like a sign! I instantly – and almost instinctively – began setting up my blog; and I remember it feeling so natural almost; because I didn't even think about a title for it – I'm NOT Disordered just sort of came to me and it felt 'right.' In all honesty, on the many occasions I've had to try and describe this beginning to my blog, I've always felt that I can never do the actual experience justice. As though convinced that no one will ever fully appreciate or understand just how apt and natural it all felt.

When my mental health was at its most poorly during those three years prior to beginning I'm NOT Disordered, I was 100% certain that I had been put on this earth to commit suicide at a young age to highlight the failings of mental health services. I was so sure that this was my destiny that it was one of a few reasons why I didn't put much effort into preventing it from coming true. So, one aspect of starting my blog which I also feel is truly inexplicable, is how reassuring it was to experience this notion that I was doing something I felt I was 'meant' to do. Finally, there was something positive and productive in my life; something which I could add to the reasons why I should be fighting to survive.

In starting to blog, I also had to confront the idea of who I wanted to see it and I immediately knew that I wanted it to be for my friends and family so I decided to only share the link to it on my private Facebook account because I had no strangers or the type of people that you say you 'sort of know.' Even that though – sharing my blog posts with my loved ones – was a huge step for me because it wasn't until just after finding out that I was being transferred to the psychiatric hospital where their 'average length of admission' is said to be 12 – 18 months. Knowing that meant I realised that if I was going to continue keeping just how terrible my mental health was a secret, I'd need to come up with an enormous lie to explain my absence for that length of time!

So, I published a post on Facebook finally talking about how the stigma surrounding mental illness had meant I had refused to talk about my own struggle, but now I was going into hospital for treatment, I felt it was time to be honest and open. I remember receiving all these 'likes' on the post and, I think, around over 20 comments from my friends and family wishing me support and reassuring me that I was brave for finally talking about things and that they were hopeful for my recovery. On the one hand, I was so emotional and overwhelmed with the love, kindness, empathy, and support I was being shown, but on the other hand, I felt absolutely terrible for even remotely debating whether they would do or be anything but that! I shouldn't have doubted them.

In deciding to only share my blog with those few people on my Facebook, I became surprised when the reader counter began to rise above my expectations, but quickly recognised that everyone was telling everyone else about it and sharing the links on their own social media which had a lot more contacts than my own. After a month or so, it was almost like I admitted defeat and I just started sharing I'm NOT Disordered on my public social media accounts too.

So, to go from having that genuinely 'small' (but extremely important) target audience, to having over one million readers is incredibly startling and overwhelmingly strange – in the best sense though! But I'm so glad to have gone about things this way because I think if you begin blogging with the hopes of having millions of readers, you could – for a number of reasons – become massively disappointed very quickly. On the other hand, should you have that hope and actually achieve it... Well, I'd imagine it would be a completely different sense of satisfaction and that it might pose the thought 'what now?'

The most difficult aspect (because – not to sound ungrateful – but, of course, there are some!) of having so many readers, for me, has been that if I were to truly concentrate on just how many people are reading what I write, I think I'd suffer from 'stage fright' and would find I had no more words! But, I do think that this challenge has helped me to stay grounded and humble because as grateful and honoured as I am to have so many readers, I actually tend not to think about it too often – I mean, of course I celebrate reader milestones, but then I go back to just focusing on what I'm writing, what I want to achieve from it, how much I want it to help others, and how much I enjoy creating my content.

2. Spend time with loved ones

Another hugely challenging factor that can come with your blog reaching milestones and experiencing achievements in its popularity and/or collaboration opportunities etc; is that you can very quickly and easily find yourself surrounded by people with different and somewhat 'wrong' priorities and motivations for wanting to be in your life.

Fortunately, I would say that I've never experienced the recognition that someone is using their relationship with me to gain mentions, publicity, or collaborations on I'm NOT Disordered. This – very obviously – doesn't mean I'm right and that no one has though! It also – equally obviously – doesn't mean that other bloggers don't seriously struggle with this challenge in creating relationships and developing trust in others when your blog is popular and successful. When I was doing a lot of media appearances, a best friend once said to me that I had the life that other people want in doing press, getting gifts from big companies, and travelling all over the country to events etc. I remember feeling so happy with that comment, but I also found myself a bit nervous at the thought that perhaps I was about to start being confronted by jealousy from others (not the best-friend who made the comment!).

There is one massively important relationship that has come since and because of my blogging career and that is with one of my best-friends and author of this book's Foreword; Martin Baker. I met Martin at a mental health event a number of years ago and since then we've grown so close; not only because he is in general an amazing person, but also because he actually has a mental health blog as well; Gum On My Shoe! This makes him the only other blogger in my circle of loved ones and that has meant he has a better understanding of this massively important feature and part to my life. Which, obviously, means a great deal to me because I've discovered that empathy and validation are hugely important and helpful qualities for my mental health. There have been so many difficult instances or decision-making moments in my blogging career that I've struggled with and have felt so alone in them because I recognise that they're issues you really need to be a blogger, to appreciate and even to just properly understand the significance of the situation. But now I have Martin, I feel so much more reassured and supported – and it's not a dig at my other loved ones; it's not that they haven't supported me – it's that they haven't been able to do so in the same way that Martin can.

For relationships with loved one's aiding you to stay humble and grounded, I think they can mostly come from having people who remind you that there was a time when you weren't a blogger, and you didn't have so many readers or followers. People who can recount memories of occasions with you where you went to events and you actually weren't there to run their social media, write a blog post about it, or give a speech or presentation. Times when you were attending and all you had to think about was how expensive drinks or tickets to it were and which filter on Snapchat looked the best! A time when it was very likely that not a whole lot of people will know of you or that if they do, it won't be because you have over one million readers on your blog and have been in the newspaper and on TV.

I have two other best-friends who I've known since before I created, I'm NOT Disordered; Lauren (who I've known since 2007) and Sophie (who I've known since 2005/6-ish!). I really love that each of them – yet has that quality in common that they keep me grounded – but also have completely different lives, attitudes, personalities, behaviours... It's nice to feel like I can have such a different friendship with each of them so that I can tell each something different or I can do something different with one than I would with the other. But yes, both are amazing reminders that just like my blog states around my mental health diagnosis – being a blogger isn't a definition of me either. Although, I'd definitely be more willing to be defined by it than I would a diagnosis!

3.   Find an activity you enjoy doing other than blogging

The thinking and thought process behind this 'step' is that in having another 'activity' it might help to put things into perspective by way of helping to show you – or remind you – that blogging is not the be all and end all. When you're passionate about an activity and truly enjoy doing it, it's almost natural that if you make a mistake or experience some sense of failure in it, your mood and behaviours will be affected.

Since I first created, I'm NOT Disordered as a psychiatric hospital inpatient, I was obviously limited as to developing hobbies or discovering new, enjoyable activities and passions. However, one of the largest reasons why I refused to go to the hospital voluntarily was because they had a strict therapeutic timetable. One that meant getting up a certain time, having a morning meeting with everyone on the ward, having Dialectical Behaviour Therapy sessions, doing back-to-back activities such as reading group, and then a reflection meeting with everyone again where we'd have to go round in a circle asking each other the best part of our day.

It was kind of monotonous (especially considering my admission lasted over two years!) and having been out of school and work for the three very poorly years prior to this admission, I was accustomed to having control over how I spent my day – particularly in so far as what time I got up and went to bed.

So, initially, I resented the staff for now dictating these things and then, when they began imposing limiting our time in which we could use our laptops, I felt so frustrated. It was hard to ignore the notion that I was being punished. Which definitely wasn't helped by the fact that if, you did self-harm on the ward, you were often made to stay in an empty room for a few days! However, as I made progress in my recovery, I found myself recognising that the thought process behind these 'rules' was largely a response to the fact that the ward specialised in those with a diagnosis of Borderline Personality Disorder (now often referred to as Emotionally Unstable Personality Disorder – EUPD) and one key 'symptom' of that was instability in mood and relationships and irrational and impulsive actions/behaviours. So, I think that the staff and professionals in general, believed that by providing a very structured routine, it would reduce or at least limit the time and opportunity to struggle, self-harm, get into arguments, and get lost in hallucinations etc.

In addition to having this timetable, another factor that got in the way of me developing other passions and interests was the fact that I was actually only in hospital because I was detained under section 3 of the 1983 Mental Health Act. **This meant that** professionals were legally allowed to use force and extreme measures to do something that was going against my will and without my permission to do so. Which also meant that if I wanted to go anywhere besides the psychiatric hospital, a psychiatrist had to fill in a form and permit every single detail of it – including how long I could go for, how many staff had to accompany me, how many units of alcohol I was allowed to drink...

So, having so much control over my freedom and life in general, meant that whilst I enjoyed the creative groups in hospital and started reading a lot, I didn't really find another interest until a few months prior to my discharge from the hospital (and so, around one year into my blogging career). It came about when I found that staff were trusting me more and more and I was feeling more and more hopeful that I had a future. So, I began looking into different methods of education whilst in the hospital and after a lot of discussion, I was granted permission to attend Creative Writing classes at the local College.

Shortly after completing the course, I was discharged but fortunately, the College also ran Distance Learning courses which could be studied no matter where in the country you were – so I could continue those when I was finally transferred to a rehabilitation unit in a psychiatric hospital closer to home. Doing all those courses meant that I found I was still really interested and enjoyed learning new things, and so, since then; I've completed a number of courses online with Centre of Excellence and FutureLearn.

In looking at the course catalogues for these websites and with my blog growing into something a lot bigger than I could have ever imagined, I found myself finally recognising my passion and interest for everything to do with the communications and marketing industry. In this recognition, I thought it might be good to start getting some more professional experience in this area and so, I began looking for relevant voluntary roles – because I accepted that my mental health (despite being completely discharged from hospital at this point) wasn't quite 100% - at least not enough to be able to commit to a paid, full-time job.

Since 2017, I've never not had a voluntary job because I found that they were useful for this step in finding an additional activity to blogging. It is in this way that I found working in this industry immediately the 'right fit' for me because it meant I had a commitment that wasn't my blog, but it was in an area where I could actually use a lot of the experience, skills, and knowledge that I've gained from blogging to help me in the voluntary roles.

I really believe that having a voluntary job alongside my blogging has helped to keep me grounded and humble because it has helped me to put a lot of things in perspective. It's meant that when I'm feeling a bit of a failure because my average daily reader count has dropped, I still have another enjoyable activity I can do that will cheer me up and leave me feeling much more positive and productive.

The Top 2 Secrets to Having a Successful Event

I'm very wary of writing content like this – where I'm talking about an amazing opportunity or special experience, but I'm highlighting difficulties you may face with that. I always worry that people will hold the belief that this is somewhat ungrateful and unappreciative, and that it's perhaps even arrogant, but this is why I wanted to create this Guide; to support the wellbeing of bloggers in a way that will also highlight to others that it isn't all about what you read on a blog or see on social media account – there's so much more to it. So much more going on in the background and behind-the-scenes.

With this attitude and insight in mind, I recognise that events can sometimes be quite challenging for someone – no matter how incredible the venue, how lovely the other guests are, and how surreal the cause for celebration is – so, here are a few tips to help make things less difficult and more smooth, exciting, and enjoyable...

1. Maintain your energy levels

Now, I don't know about you, but sometimes I'll reach a point with hunger or tiredness where I'll kind of go past them and actually completely stop being hungry and/or tired. Instead, I typically end up feeling as though I'm running on adrenaline at events because I also somehow almost always find myself still having lots of work to do when there's a break or just as the food is being served!

In all honesty, I'm definitely someone who gets 'hangry' (angry when I'm hungry) and I 100% snap easily and bite people's heads off for silly reasons when I'm shattered. So, it's really important that I maintain my energy levels at events to avoid any awkward or tense moments with others and to ensure I don't struggle with carrying out my duties or feel stressed with the sheer size of my workload. With this recognition in mind, I'm now overly cautious of the amount of sleep I get prior to the event, and I'm incredibly aware of ensuring I eat something and have a drink throughout the day/event.

Aside from my mood and the more psychological side effects to me having low energy levels, there's also the practical – and arguably more important – impact too. Being irritable and tired can very easily and understandably lead to me experiencing tension with others at the event and result in work of a poor quality (on my part).

Feeling that my work isn't up to a decent standard for my readers is something I generally struggle with the idea of, so when it's related to an event (that is likely hosted by someone else) it becomes even more challenging. It means that I develop the thoughts and feelings that I'm not worthy of whatever reward or benefit I receive from the event organiser in return for doing this work.

This – maintaining my energy levels and recognising the importance of doing so – has been yet another skill or lesson I've had to learn the hard way over the years of my blogging career. So, similarly to most others that I've experienced in this way, I wanted to try to ensure that less people are having to go through such hardships in order to gain this knowledge and understanding.

2. Let yourself really be 'in the moment'

When I began Dialectical Behaviour Therapy (DBT) as a psychiatric hospital inpatient in 2012, and I first heard of 'Mindfulness' and that it was an entire module in the Therapy, I was immediately sceptical and incredibly hesitant to take part in it. My very brief understanding of it from the staff's introduction was that it was all about 'being in the moment.' There was different calming, relaxing and breathing exercises you could use to help to do this and firstly, those sorts of coping mechanisms don't appeal to me in general.

Then there was the additional motivation for my reluctance to engage in the Mindfulness module of the fact that I 100% believed and was confident that if I allowed my mind and body to be 'in the moment' I would pretty much end up even more suicidal. I felt this way because I was certain that one of the greatest methods, I've used in keeping myself as safe as possible has been doing something that will lead to me forgetting or really distancing myself from whatever I'm experiencing that's leaving me feeling so unsafe.

After two and a half years of DBT (which meant going through the Mindfulness module at least twice) I started to come round to its presence and recognise that it could be adapted to fit better with me and my mental health in a way that would make it more efficient and affective. So, I started practicing Mindfulness when I do something fun or if I have a real one-off, special opportunity/experience.

The first time I really used the DBT skill in this way was when I hosted a large party to celebrate my blog; I'm NOT Disordered reaching 100,000 readers. It was at the end of the party, there was only me, my Mum, and two of my best-friends there, and the musician I'd hired was still playing his guitar. So, Sophie (one of the best-friends) asked him to play Mr Brightside by The Killers and the three of us hit the dancefloor! I remember closing my eyes and putting my arms out and twirling around and just... Putting all my concentration into remembering every single detail about that moment.

Having the amazing thoughts and feelings I experienced in that moment almost carved into my memories, has meant that even around seven or eight years later, it's still one of the greatest nights of my life. The very real, genuine, and truly overwhelming feeling of pride I had with the recognition that this entire event was due to my own hard work, and the sense of support and love I felt from those two best friends has never been forgotten or unappreciated.

"Networking isn't how many people you know, it's how many people know you"

Amit Kalantri

Why I Decided to Do Media Interviews & Appearances

When I first created my blog; I'm NOT Disordered in 2013, it was with the goal of helping my loved ones to gain better insight into – not just my personal journey – but also, mental health both in general, and on a larger scale too. To ensure that my blogs content was reaching those loved ones, I only shared the link to it on my private Facebook account where I truly have actual friends and family; but I think that word-of-mouth took hold because before I knew it, the size of my readership was growing to a degree that was very obviously beyond an amount of people I actually knew!

As the statistics began to soar, I found myself faced with an almost automatic, predictable decision to make as to whether I wanted things to continue this way. Whether I wanted to actually start making a conscious effort to attract more readers to my blog. However, before I could even really think that through, I found myself receiving a ton of benefits from having so many readers.

My favourite two benefits to my blog's popularity have firstly been that it helps in assuring prospective collaboration partners that they'll really be rewarded (particularly in terms of publicity and marketing) in working with I'm NOT Disordered. Initially, this was a notion that I didn't enjoy because I felt it a bit of a sign that prioritising the number of views and followers, they would gain from working with myself and my blog, felt like a sign that the prospective collaborator wasn't doing it for the right reasons.

Over the years of blogging, I have been asked on numerous occasions whether I get paid for doing it. I usually tell people that

I'm often gifted items or given discount codes, but mostly I do a lot of my collaboration work without any sort of financial gain; except where accommodation and travel costs are concerned – I typically ask the partner to cover the cost of those elements. In answering this question, I also like to add that I don't claim expenses or offer advertorial places on my blog because I don't want readers to think I'm doing all of this for the wrong reasons. I don't want people to feel confident in saying that I'm not genuine or that I have the wrong priorities and motivations.

Now, I'd like to think that those who know me, would never make a comment like that – and that, if anything, they would actually stick up for me should someone else make such a comment in their presence. Complete strangers – or general members of the public – however, have become so conditioned to pretty much just assuming that every blogger must be making money from their content because there are so many bloggers and online influencers out there who really emphasise in different ways in their content that they do make money from their blogging and content creation.

In fairness, I completely appreciate that people need to make a living, and everyone has bills to pay – believe me; I most definitely appreciate that! – I just worry that in mental health blogging earning money in some way would give the impression that I'm not entirely dedicated or passionate about my content. As though I only produce some posts because I'm paid to. Some might say "who cares what other people think? As long as you know that's not why you do this…" But for me – and in this instance in particular – it's challenging to just not care about the judgment of others. Especially when they're so wrong and where these opinions can actually lead to a really hugely negative impact on my reputation and on my blog's name too.

The final of my two favourite benefits to the size of my blog's readership it that it has given me a greater chance and/or opportunity for my content to help others. In all honesty, if someone were to ask me my most favourite moment in my blogging career, yes, I would struggle to pick just one, but I imagine that in the end, I would say that it happened a few years ago. A little while ago, I had published a blog post about reporting abuse to the Police and the process I went through, ways to cope etc when I got an email from a reader.

In this email, the reader told me that she had been abused at a young age by a family member and that – like me – for so many reasons, she hadn't reported it to the Police. However, she said, that after reading my blog post and how terrified I had been in reporting the abuse, but how much closure I had gained from doing so; she found the courage, determination, and dedication to fight for her own rights and to get justice for what had been done to her too. So, she called the Police.

That alone felt hugely powerful, but when the reader went on to write that her abuser had been immediately arrested, more people had come forward to accuse him of abusing them too, and so, the Crown Prosecution Service (CPS) deemed there to be enough evidence to take the abuser to court. Which is why the reader had taken some time since I published the post because she wanted to hear the court verdict before emailing me. Her abuser was found guilty and sentenced to jail time.

Alongside being unable to believe that a rapist and sexual abuser had actually been given time in prison – because, let's face it, when do they ever get a justifiable punishment/consequent from the courts – I also couldn't believe the fact that my little blog and the post I had written, had such a huge, life-changing impact on a reader.

The more I thought about that though, I actually ended up feeling quite terrible for not recognising sooner the influence and power my blog posts had over the thousands of readers I'm

NOT Disordered was gaining every day. I thought that it meant I had been so incredibly naïve because I had been blogging for a number of years by this point, so I found myself really questioning why it hadn't occurred to me sooner. Of course, I had received emails and comments about how my content had helped someone in various ways with their mental health; whether that meant by teaching someone a new safe and healthy coping skill or encouraging them to seek help from various mental health support services I've partnered with. But I think that when something is said to you so often and over and over again, it can very sadly lose its meaning and importance. So, whilst I greatly appreciate and want to encourage readers to share with me when my content has helped their mental health in some way; no one had ever told me my posts had impacted their life to the gravity of it helping to jail a predator so that many others are also protected.

I would like to say though, the fact my blog has impacted someone, doesn't and shouldn't take away from the fact that a person has to want help or has to be willing to take advice in order to benefit from I'm NOT Disordered's content. So, my words could very easily fall on deaf ears; but if you find them helpful, that says a lot of good, positive things about you.

Experiencing these incredible impacts that the popularity of my blog has made available or afforded me, has really helped to motivate me to find the confidence and willing to work with the media and to talk about my blog more publicly.

How To Decide If You Should Work with The Media

As with many aspects of blogging, deciding whether to work with the media is very much an individual consideration where the benefits and drawbacks of doing it, can massively differ between various blogs/bloggers. So, it's important that you really tailor your consideration and making the decision as to whether you should work with the media to be relevant to yourself and your own blog; but here are some general points that are worth keeping in mind...

1. How would you feel if you were asked a question you didn't want to answer?

2. Can you cope with any backlash from the media's audience (which will likely be larger than your blog's)?

3. What would you do if the media edited your interview/appearance into a way you didn't like?

4. How will you cope with the possible positive and negative impacts your media appearance could have?

5. How would you decide which press outlets you'd like to work with and which you wouldn't?

Managing Your Anxiety in Public Speaking

Across my blogging career, I have learnt – on many occasions – that you don't have to have a diagnosis of an anxiety disorder; or even be someone that typically struggles with anxiety, in order to experience it in blogging scenarios such as hosting an event, delivering a presentation, and speaking to the media. Personally, anxiety isn't something I've ever really struggled with, and I'd stand firm on this, especially since witnessing other psychiatric hospital inpatients have panic attacks and need some sort of sedative medication due to their anxiety and its de-stabilising impact on their mental health and then – because of that – their safety too.

I am, however, mindful, of the notion that comparing your mental health (or anything in life, really) to another person's isn't always fair or productive. You can end up dismissing your own difficulties or viewing them as unimportant and unworthy of reaching out for help and support. Doing this, can have the very real consequence of things only worsening to a point where you definitely need help and that help, and support takes a lot longer to make a difference.

So, with that in mind, I'd say that I've felt anxious a number of times in my blogging career; but never to the point where I've needed help or treatment for it. One of the most anxious aspects of being a blogger and doing everything I do with my blog, has been public speaking. Now, I recognise that this is really a completely optional part to working in this industry or having a career like this – which is why I talked about making the decision to do these things – but for me, it has massively felt like the right step in my blogging. So, I don't want it to sound as though I'm moaning about something I've chosen to do; I'd rather it be seen as me talking about managing your wellbeing in doing this, as an opportunity to provide better insight and understanding for both those who either have no experience of this or those who are deciding whether to or not to do this.

Now, I'm very much one for jumping in at the deep end so my first public speaking occasion was delivering the closing speech for Story Camp with Time to Change in a huge auditorium and with hundreds of people there! I honestly think that I just didn't think things through until I was at the event (in London) and almost in tears with the nerves and anxiety. I remember ringing my Mum and she said, "you can do it!" So, I went ahead with the speech and actually, I really enjoyed the adrenaline rush I got from it! It was amazing to have found that courage – with the help of my Mum – to continue with the speech and then receive some really lovely feedback from people, as well as a round of applause!

Having experienced that huge sense of achievement, I continued to accept offers of public speaking and I'm now at the point where I'll often actually nominate myself and ask if I can do it!

The Inevitable Invasion of Privacy

Unfortunately, there are a lot of very real and terrible consequences and repercussions to being in the digital world; and particularly, to talking about your mental health on a blog with over one million readers! You know, there have been so many instances where a person someone I'm talking to finds out I have a blog and makes a comment around how I'm making myself vulnerable to online bullying and negative responses. But I think that this issue is somewhat similar to when people talk about how much unsafe content there can be online that it can inspire hugely dangerous actions/reactions. When I hear this comment or discussion, I will usually voice my view that the internet shows you what you want from it. If you search for content around methods of self-harm, then that's what you'll find. If you search for positive stories of mental health recovery, you'll find that too.

So, my thought process here is that if you use the internet and your social media or blog as a platform or an opportunity to voice controversial thoughts and opinions; then you really are opening yourself up to equally controversial responses or disagreements that can be posted by aggressive individuals who may not voice their own opinions calmly. Don't get me wrong; I find this really sad. A really sad fact that just naturally – and almost compulsively – comes with taking part in the digital world. I 100% believe that it shouldn't be this way – I just realise, accept, and recognise that it is.

With all of this in mind, a loss of privacy when you're a blogger or online influencer seems equally likely, understandable, and predictable too. When I first started blogging, because my target audience was just my friends and family on my private Facebook account, I didn't stop and take any sort of time or put any effort into considering just how much detail I would go into on my blog posts about my life and, obviously, about my mental health in particular. This meant that when I noticed the number of readers begin to climb and move to way beyond the amount of people I had in my life, I felt I couldn't change this and suddenly become private and limit what I talked about and the details I went into on my blog posts. Mostly because I was convinced that the reader growth meant people must like my content. So, I thought that if I altered the fundamental elements to that in any way, I would risk things going backwards and a decline in my audience, which would mean a reduction in the amount of people my content could help.

My thought process has, so far, turned out right because the most honest and open posts on I'm NOT Disordered, end up being the most popular and the most likely to trigger lovely feedback from readers. From observing so many interactions in the digital world, I think that a really big contribution for readers love for honesty comes from the recognition that absolutely everyone who uses social media, only posts what they want others to see. This mostly means that you'll see the positives – the holidays, the nights out, the events, the collaborations, gifted experiences, the freebies... Then, the difficult moments, the tears, the travel dramas, the mistakes, the late nights and early mornings, aren't publicised.

In all honesty – whilst I do the exact opposite – I have no real qualm with influencers and bloggers who do this because I appreciate that it's incredibly likely that their motto or goal in posting such content is to bring some sort of positive emotion to their followers/readers/subscribers. For all I – or anyone else – knows those creators could very well be struggling with doing this and they might be debating the idea of actually starting to talk about the entirety of their life.

In seeing other bloggers and influencers stay private and measure how personal their content is, it's helped me to better understand why one of my loved ones is so guarded in anything I put on social media or on I'm NOT Disordered that's either related to – or even subtly mentions – them. Prior to recognising those others who have made a career out of the digital world, I actually genuinely didn't understand this person's very cautious attitude. This was particularly because this person has gone through a few massive hardships that I honestly believe – if they were to share their journey on a public platform/media in some way – they could actually help a lot of others.

In addition to recognising others with a similar attitude, I've also looked on this as a bit of a respect issue in that this person has requested privacy and they mean so much to me that I feel I should respect that. I realise that this person didn't sign up to have their life plastered across my social media or I'm NOT Disordered – that was me and my decision. It really comes down to being largely about treating others how you want to be treated, so I think people should respect the decision of others as much and as equal as you would like your own to be.

The other, more recent challenge I've faced around my privacy has been a bit more obvious and understandable because it was around my media appearances. In deciding to work with the various forms of media (I've featured in newspaper articles, magazine stories, on the local news, the national news, a documentary, and on the radio), I focused on the idea that sharing my mental health journey could provide a sense of hope for others to see that I've gone from being so suicidal that I was on life support, to where/who I am today. I also thought that talking in the media about my blog, could encourage others to join this industry – which is something I'd like to do because being a blogger has helped me/my mental health so much that I'd really like to think it could do the same for others.

So, with these two massive motivations for my media appearances in mind, I've found them so powerful that I've managed to cope with the experiences and notions of these appearances invading my privacy. I think that the most difficult instance regarding this issue, was when I was being interviewed in my home for a news piece on TV, and the interviewer kept pushing me to disclose the details of the person who had abused me. I felt quite fortunate that I couldn't tell her because of legal reasons because otherwise, she honestly probably would have worn me down!

Finally, alongside my motivations for being in the media, I also recognise that fundamentally, I've chosen to do this. I've chosen to create a blog and to make it into all that it is today. I chose to start appearing in the media. I chose to let those reasons and motivations for doing so, to be as powerful and meaningful as they are. So, in me, it initiates the idea of making my own bed and lying in it. Who am I to complain or voice my struggles when I've put myself in this situation? In total contradiction to that, I think that actually, I need to be more grateful for the fact that I have control over a huge amount of this – I can decide when things are going too far or getting a bit much. I can edit my blog posts and decide on just how my social media posts are phrased.

Managing Intimidating Sized Pressure & Expectations

In going so public with my mental health recovery and my blog's journey, in addition to the loss of privacy, I've also experienced a huge battle with the subsequent increase in expectations, pressures, power, and influence related not just to I'm NOT Disordered but to myself as a blogger too.

When I first began blogging in 2013, I would have never imagined being where I – and my blog – is today; and a huge part of that unbelievable quality, comes with the recognition of the power and influence my blog; I'm NOT Disordered, can have – particularly during collaborations. Having initially started blogging with the hope of simply communicating my thoughts, feelings, and behaviours better, I didn't envisage that it'd end up capable of impacting all those qualities in its readers too!

I like to think that this – the fact I didn't start blogging with the aspiration to secure gifted items, to have the ability to associate my blog's name with a huge organisation, or to be awarded with complimentary experiences – brings a more genuine, passionate, and dedicated element to my blog, its content, and its collaborations.

These days, with bloggers becoming so infamous for their freebies that are worth thousands and their constant barrage of advertorial content, it's difficult to recognise exactly what a person's motivation is for joining this industry. Where everyone is so very aware of the material benefits available to bloggers, how can you really look at someone who is just joining the industry and be filled with the confidence and certainty that they're doing so purely because they find it therapeutic or genuinely helpful in some similar or equivalently wholesome way?

As I talked about earlier, I always pride myself and I'm NOT Disordered's content on being open and honest; so of course, I won't lie and pretend that I don't really appreciate and enjoy the complimentary experiences I've had the opportunity of engaging in, and the gifted products and items I've received. Of course, I have! And, of course I've made the most of these extremely rewarding elements that typically come with a collaboration. But I've done so because that's how I see them; as rewards for all the time and effort I've put into creating the content – whether that means taking and editing photos, creating graphics or other visual resources via Canva, writing lengthy blog posts, putting reels together, collecting and publishing links, and finding other pieces of relevant information.

Something that's really important to me around publishing posts that could be understandably referred to as advertorial are that I always make sure whatever it is I'm blogging about is relevant to my blog's theme of mental health. Whilst I sometimes have to be incredibly creative to make that happen/be possible, I like to think I keep things genuine and never post something that I believe no one will find helpful. I do this because I fully recognise the very surreal level of powerful influence that myself/I'm NOT Disordered holds with its multitude of readers. I can very easily appreciate that you can come to trust the opinion and recommendation of online influencers and bloggers – particularly when you've been a follower or reader of their content for some time (and I've been blogging for over a decade now so there's a very real possibility that I have some amazing readers who have been here for a huge part of this insane journey!).

Throughout the most recent years of the growth and development of I'm NOT Disordered, I have created a Media Kit for instances where I'm pitching a collaboration or partnership project of some sort. When I started designing it on Canva, and researched what others include in their own, I learnt the statistics of how beneficial my blog has been for collaboration partners e.g., up to a 79% increase for charities and up to a 3,000 increase in social media following for all organisations. Finding this out was partly incredibly rewarding and gave a huge notion of achievement, but it was also really intimidating in that I felt so much more self-conscious than ever of the words I use and the way I phrase even the most trivial or minor things.

I think that the reason for the difficult feelings around this recognition of the impact my blog can have in collaborations stemmed from the recognition that if these statistics were to decline in some/any way, I was the only person responsible for that. This meant that it would literally be 100% my fault if a collaboration went wrong and underperformed in failing to meet these statistics for the partnering organisation. In all honesty, I find it quite sad that something which really is a huge achievement, can have some massive drawbacks that I might end up actually struggling to cope with. It's a lot of pressure.

However, I have chosen to do this, and I've chosen to put so much time and effort into making my blog into being capable of reaching these accomplished statistics... So again, what right do I have to moan or complain? I'd like to think, however, that people recognise that for a lot of bloggers and influencers, we actually don't often start out with the vision – or even intention – of becoming all that we become and all that we subsequently experience due to this.

Now that blogging is more popular and talked about a lot more in the media and amongst the public in general, I feel that a lot of people can enter the industry with a pretty decent idea or appreciation of the challenges they might go on to face depending upon the work they put in and the quality and popularity of the content they go on to produce.

Back in 2013 however – when I started blogging – the industry wasn't even an industry! Those of us who were in it, were sort of making it up as we went along; and so, I had no real clue as to the impact and affect the content I created and the decisions I made about my blog would have long-term. I didn't even envision a 'long-term' timeline to be fair! Having started blogging with the largest motivation of wanting to better communicate my journey in the psychiatric hospital over 100 miles away from home to my loved ones; meant that I genuinely assumed my blogging wouldn't go any further after being discharged from the hospital. So, in those early months, I didn't really consider long-term consequences to my actions and decisions around I'm NOT Disordered.

With my genuine lack of insight into any sort of future for my blog, the pressure and expectations have been seriously difficult, upsetting, and incredibly overwhelming too! I think I've managed these challenging thoughts and feelings by finding the confidence that I can't be doing too poorly to have the number of readers I have and the standard of organisations and people I get to collaborate with. I also keep in mind that at every decision-making moment, I'm doing my best. I'm honestly making the decisions and taking the actions that I believe are the best for myself and for my readers. So I recognise that as long as I always remember this, what more can I do?

"There are so many people who will tell you that you can't do this, but you have to make sure that your voice isn't one of them"

Pooja Agnilhotri

The Trolls

Similarly, to the fact that posting anything on social media can make you instantly susceptible to an onslaught of alternative opinions, thoughts, and experiences; a large downside to my honesty about my mental health was that it could very easily leave me wide open to the prospect of some really nasty online bullying – or 'trolling.' In all honesty, I 100% believe this is so completely wrong, but it is reality. A very sad and damaging, or potentially life-threatening, reality.

Online bullying is something which has pretty much been around since the online world was founded and became more accessible to the general public! I mean, if you're going to create a forum where people can express their opinions, you're pretty much equally enabling disagreements, arguments, negativity, spitefulness, and competition.

When I was fifteen and going through the abuse, I had a number of reasons why I couldn't report what was happening to me to the Police or to anyone really. So, I began acting out at school – for two reasons... Firstly, in the hope that a teacher would sit up and say, "this isn't like Aimee, maybe something's going on?" Secondly, when that wasn't happening, it then became out of anger and frustration that no one seemed to care enough to realise or to step in and ask if I was ok. So, I took their neglect and the absence of their care and thought as an annoying insult. I felt at a complete loss as to what else I could do to bring attention to the matter without sitting there and blurting it out for everyone to hear. For everyone to judge.

Of course, it wasn't just the teachers who seemed ignorant or reluctant to make any effort to actually consider the cause or deeper meaning behind my complete change in attitude and behaviour; the other pupils – including my friends – didn't either.

Instead, they began bullying me for being an 'attention-seeker' and a 'drama queen.' They bullied me for behaviours they didn't even remotely bother to try and understand.

I was already feeling so lonely with the idea that I was the only person in the world being hurt by this... 'man.' In all honesty, I thought I was the only person being hurt full stop. I had no real awareness of education of abuse and rape and so I had no knowledge of just how frequently it occurs and how many people are affected by it. So, to have my 'friends' turn on me was horrible and when their comments went beyond being at school and they turned to MSN Messenger to call me a 'bag of bones' and 'worthless' I felt that there was no escape. They could now get to me even from the safety of my home.

I can't remember finally telling my Mum, but I do remember my abuser lining them up in his office and shouting at them to stop it. When that worked, he made out like I owed him for doing it. For doing what was right and what anyone with the power to, should do.

I recognise some horrible comments online by people who you thought were friends doesn't sound that horrific compared to the media stories you hear about trolling and bullying online these days – especially where it's resulted in suicide. However, I think everyone's experiences of this issue should be regarded and recognised as important to that person. For me, this experience has always remained a part of my memory and so my opinions when talking about the digital world and social media. In a way, I'm glad for it because it's meant I have a much more balanced view of this industry – I can appreciate both the positive and the criticisms of it that different people hold and believe in. However, I do believe that this experience would have been more than 'enough' to provide me with this insight! There was no need for the additional instances I've experienced in my blogging career!

You're NOT Disordered

Now, there were three instances of horrible comments early in starting I'm NOT Disordered, but the one that I paid the most attention to and which was the most debilitating was around a blog post focused on World Suicide Prevention Day. In the post, I had talked about my two experiences of making a suicide attempt and then came an anonymous comment that read 'good luck with the third.'

I think that a huge part of my upset in receiving this, was in the actual nature of the comment as opposed to being more about the personal aspect of it... Like, the most important thing was the fundamental side of the comment – the meaning and definition behind it – rather than the fact it was actually sent to me. I would have been horrified to read it had been sent to absolutely anyone else too! In my opinion, to encourage someone to kill yourself is unforgivable.

It actually reminds me of this time when I was in a psychiatric hospital and another inpatient snuck a blade onto the ward from their leave and it was passed around the other patients. Staff finally realised when they saw everyone had similar injuries and someone finally handed it in. I wasn't part of it. I was actually on the staff's 'team' in completely condemning the whole notion of it. Even if I've found self-harm temporarily helpful, I would never encourage someone to use it as a coping mechanism. I just don't know why you would want someone to feel that way or to go through anything remotely similar to what you have experienced when you've done it.

When I received this comment and the two others, they were actually around the time I was being transferred from the psychiatric hospital, so I made the decision to close I'm NOT Disordered down, and I stopped blogging. It felt sort of poignant to close that chapter of my life in unison with my transfer to the psychiatric hospital nearer home.

Within months, though, I found myself missing the outlet and with me still being in a psychiatric hospital – except a much more open and less strict one – I found that I still had a lot of thoughts and experiences going on that I felt the need to really still write/type about. Getting back into blogging on I'm NOT Disordered, the fact that my mental health had drastically improved since I had first created it over one year ago and having gone through the horrible comments; I was a lot more guarded and sensible in what I posted/published. I massively stayed clear of anything even remotely controversial, and I kept my content 100% personal, honest, and open so that I felt confident in the notion that no one could really challenge it or disagree without looking foolish.

I also saw an additional, beneficial, more helpful aid to me fighting off any horrible comments and trolling by continuing with my collaborations and networking opportunities. I recognised – and found myself to be right – that having the 'backing' and support of others who stand high and important in the community or in society on a whole; can give added weight to my defence or opinion/experience. It's not about wanting to be intimidating, I really see it as a huge bonus to doing something I really enjoy (collaborations and partnership content). Though, in keeping with my typical honesty, I won't lie that being able to say that I have worked alongside the Chief Executive of such-and-such organisation, or the Inspector of such-and-such Police Force can be hugely beneficial and supportive in helping me feel capable of facing any undue or unfair backlash or trolling.

Of course, in coming up against trolls and online bullying, I'd always recommend that you seek professional help and support if you come to feel unsafe and at risk. It might also be useful to seek reassurance and comradery in speaking with other bloggers or online influencers who may have overcome similar difficulties and be able to really understand and appreciate how you're feeling and what you're going through.

Beware Of the Jealousy & Copycats

When I created my blog; I'm NOT Disordered on January 6th, 2013, I do so with really only three well-known mental health blogs. One was written by a Police Officer with an interest in mental health law, another was by an ex-psychiatric hospital inpatient, and the third was created by a psychiatric Nurse. I struggled to find any written by an actual, current, psychiatric hospital inpatient. Seeing the extremely saturated blogging world now and the amount of mental health blogs there are, I feel so very lucky and extremely fortunate to have almost naturally and accidentally found a niche for my blog without even really trying.

I recognise that having some sort of stand-out quality to your blog and an aspect about it that's dissimilar to any currently out there in the digital world. However, I also recognise that this really depends upon your goals for your blog... I mean, if you don't intend to earn any large number of readers or followers or if you aren't keen to work with charities and organisations in collaboration content, then I guess it really doesn't matter how common your blog's aesthetic, purpose, meaning, persona, and even its content is. If you're doing this purely for yourself and have no other motive...

The irony is, whilst I had that niche straight away in my blogging career, I actually was still one of those people (who have no real huge dreams or intentions and goals in mind in so far as the size of their blog's audience etc) because I really started, I'm NOT Disordered as an outlet and a communication method. The psychiatric hospital I was a sectioned (detained under the 1983 Mental Health Act) patient in was over 100 miles away from my home, my friends, and my family. The reason for this, was that it was the nearest one which specialised in my diagnosis of Borderline Personality Disorder (BPD) and would accept my flight risk!

Being so far away from the town I'd spent almost my entire life and from the people – especially my Mum – who I'd grown up with and built amazing relationships and friendships with, wasn't actually that difficult at first. This, I think, was because my mental health was so poorly that I didn't really register the distance; all my mind would focus on was the suicidal thoughts, feelings, and plans. I had no real room in my head for anything else and I was so cut off from any positive emotions or thoughts for other people that I didn't miss anyone until after a few months into my admission and so I created I'm NOT Disordered.

My other motivation for starting to blog was because I had always found writing to be a really positive and productive outlet for my creativity, thoughts, feelings, and experiences. When I was little it was more about writing short stories about adventures with horses (I used to go horse-riding when I was younger) and then, when my mental health deteriorated, it became more about communicating how I was thinking and what I was feeling to mental health professionals in a way that felt more efficient and effective than talking ever would be. I struggled to find the words when it came to therapy sessions and being asked questions but give me a pen and paper – or a laptop with a keyboard! – and I'd be pouring my heart out!

I'd like to think that having such innocent and pure hopes and motivations for the beginning of I'm NOT Disordered really helped set it in good stead in terms of attracting readers and interest from those who might be interested in collaborating. I believe that was important because in addition to there now being a great deal of blogs written by people with BPD and those in psychiatric hospitals, the motivation and attraction to join the blogging industry has also changed to a point where it leads to question the sincerity and honesty of a blogger's content. With collaborations and partnership content being so hugely influential and taking the shape of free stays in 5* hotels, free flights abroad, complimentary products, and items of expensive, designer clothing; it can lend itself to being the reason for someone to create a blog.

These two fundamental aspects of blogging – the reason for you entering the industry and the difference of your blog/content to that which already exists/is published – can be the absolute cornerstones of how successful (in terms of popularity and the size and span of your audience) your blog becomes/is. It is from this, that jealousy and copycats are born... Because any sort of achievement or accomplishment can very easily be something which others were/are either striving for themselves or would ideally like to be in that same position or at that same milestone.

Talking about jealousy, for me, typically brings up that saying about 'the grass is always greener on the other side.' I think that this is mostly because of the very well-known and obvious fact that so many online influencers don't publish content that in any way reflects anything negative or difficult about their life and especially anything challenging that is even remotely in the remit of being connected to their career as an influencer or blogger. In all honesty, whilst I appreciate those who do this will have their rationale and motive and reasons for doing so, I can't quite comprehend what they might be. I think this is because it's very obviously the complete opposite method and mindset to my own creation of content.

I think that the one thought process I can grasp is that fashion, beauty, and travel bloggers might argue that there is no real necessity for them to talk about – or post about – any difficult, personal moments in their life because that's not why people visit their blog or their social media accounts. People aren't going to them neither looking for, nor expecting, that type of content. This might also raise the point or argument that perhaps if a blogger doesn't produce content of that personal, sensitive, and vulnerable nature then perhaps that will mean it's not something they would do well. I mean, I have a big passion for fashion and beauty – in fact I follow more blogs of that genre than I do of mental health! – but I 100% recognise that I might not be the best person to produce a blog post or social media content on the topics.

Herein, lies another reason or cause for jealousy – the recognition that another blogger or influencer is more experienced and talented or skilled at writing about a particular subject that another might wish they could write at the same level/of the same quality. I actually have a best friend who also has a mental health blog (www.gumonmyshoe.com) and he is incredibly knowledgeable in grammar and the very intense technicalities of writing – something I'm not so familiar with because I feel as though I just write how I would speak. This is why I'm uncomfortable to accept when people have commented that I have a 'natural gift' in writing because I don't feel as though I try that hard... I guess that's the point of the comment though?! Mind you, I've certainly put a lot of thought, effort, and time into writing this Guide because I recognise it needs a more formal narrative than I would typically use in my blog's content.

Aside from believing others are 'better' than you at something which you love just the mere thought of being able to do, another cause for jealousy or copying can be in instances when you're hitting some significant and/or special milestones in both your blogging career and your blog's existence (because I fully believe these can be two separate entities). It's a bit of a Catch-22 here because I'm definitely one for wanting to mark and celebrate milestones in I'm NOT Disordered and my work more generally in this industry; however, I do recognise that doing so can really open you up to a lot of rivalry and hostility.

Prior to my blogging career and in the early years after creating I'm NOT Disordered, I was never one to blow my own trumpet, but I've gained so much confidence in doing this sort of thing through my blog. This is largely born from the recognition that in order to better my blog and its content, I've found that it's almost necessary – and can only really be achieved – if you're willing to plug it (your blog) and yourself/your social media accounts. However, whilst I say it was a few years into having my blog before I did this, that doesn't mean it took me that long to learn or to realise that I needed to do it!

It actually didn't take me too long at all because it was fairly early on that I realised how positive it was for me, and how beneficial it felt for me to see my audience grow and grow. The notion that these were added individuals that I had the opportunity to help or impact in some way (obviously, hopefully in a positive sense!) meant a lot to me. Then, in recognising this, I came to the joint conclusion that to make the increase in the size of I'm NOT Disordered's readership happen, collaborations with well-known people and organisations are extremely helpful and productive.

In gaining more and more readers and being able to say that I had successfully landed some collaborations with people and organisations that I felt were really important and special in their own right, I found the confidence to really enjoy and celebrate milestones. I recognised that they were massive illustrations of my hard work and all the time I was putting into creating all the content I publish. The meaning of occasions such as my blog's ten year Birthday and reaching one million readings was so intense and so special that I also found the confidence to go ahead and shout about them at risk of others showing spiteful jealousy.

Unfortunately – but, in my opinion, understandably – jealousy in the blogging industry can very quickly and easily lead to a ton of copying. Copying of content theme, of the aesthetic and design of the blog, of the process in creating the content, of the layout of blog posts, of the narrative and voice given to the content...

The challenging issue here is ensuring that the difference between copying and inspiration or influence is registered and established. I will honestly say that I have been massively inspired by other bloggers in so far as the themes of their content. This has typically been where a blogger or online influencer has written about a topic that I find relevant or important to myself too and where I feel it would be beneficial for myself and/or I'm NOT Disordered's readers to share my own thoughts, feelings, and experiences on it in a blog post. In my content of this nature, I've also always referenced and credited the blogger/blog that has been so influential on it. I do this because this is how I would like to be treated and acknowledged if someone were to take inspiration from my content.

There's been numerous occasions when I've talked about wanting to encourage people to join the blogging industry and I've actually ended up being questioned as to why I would welcome more people who would have the potential to attract readers away from I'm NOT Disordered. My response has always been that blogging has helped me and my mental health so much that I absolutely love the thought that it has the potential to do the same for someone else. For me, this notion of being a part of someone's mental health, or their life in general, improving is so important to me – more so than the idea that doing so, might reduce the size of my blog's audience. I'd so much rather inspire hope and positivity by talking about the benefits of blogging than influence competitiveness and jealousy by making a conscious effort not to promote it nor to encourage others to try blogging too.

"It was impossible, of course. But when did that ever stop any dreamer from dreaming?"

Laini Taylor

Why I Started Creating Goals for I'm NOT Disordered

In this final section of the Guide, I wanted to talk about goals which are something that's more about long-term blogging and is more relevant to bloggers who are a lot more dedicated and driven to their blog as a career rather than those in the industry who would deem theirs to be more of a hobby or something to fill their spare time.

Thinking on it, I've obviously had an awareness or understanding of setting goals in terms of having deadlines for school homework and essays etc. or completing my duties in the weekend job I had at a retail store. However, my first real experience of setting a more meaningful and arguably more important goal was in therapy after my mental health had deteriorated.

I had made a suicide attempt in June 2012 and after being on life support in Intensive Care, I was sectioned under the 1983 Mental Health Act and admitted to a specialist psychiatric hospital. Specialising in my diagnosis of Borderline Personality Disorder (BPD) meant that the hospital provided the recommended treatment for BPD; Dialectical Behaviour Therapy (DBT – yes, the mental health world is full of abbreviations!), and in groups and 1:1 sessions we were given 'homework' and a number of times this meant recording some goals for yourself and your general wellbeing. This could mean anything from aiming to not self-harm for the week between therapy sessions to making sure you eat three meals a day for that duration to wanting to use at least two DBT skills every day for the week!

In all honesty, it didn't take much convincing or pointing out to me for me to believe that setting goals was a really good move –

especially in/for your mental health and wellbeing. I immediately found that I really enjoyed creating them, working towards them, and obviously completing or achieving them. However, I also recognised straight away that to 'fail' or, for some reason, be short of reaching my goal meant I'd need to use the DBT coping skills to maintain my safety by making a conscious effort to not become hopeless or feel like a complete failure and deem DBT to be pointless.

Having started DBT in the summer of 2012, it meant that when I created my blog; I'm NOT Disordered January 6th, 2013, I had some knowledge, understanding, and experience of creating goals, but I didn't see blogging as too important or long-term. Going into the specialist hospital, I was told that the average length of admission was 12 – 18 months because one round of DBT should take 12 months (I ended up being an inpatient for two and a half years) so I knew I wasn't going to be discharged too soon after the January, but I still held it in my head that I was likely just going to blog either a couple of times and give up or forget about or that I would continue until I was discharged from the hospital. With this lack of vision for much of a future for I'm NOT Disordered, I didn't consider creating blogging goals until after I was discharged from the hospital in December 2014.

In around late Summer in 2014, I received a few horrible comments on my blog and its content and so I actually did stop blogging upon my discharge. However, within months I found myself really missing having this outlet and platform where I could talk about and process my thoughts, feelings, and experiences and so, in October 2014, I recommenced my blogging and found myself starting to envision and feel the need to begin preparing, planning, and working to have the positive, productive, and creative, long-term future that I had finally begun to envision for I'm NOT Disordered.

How To Use SMART To Create A Blogging Goal

There are so many aspects of blogging – and especially blogs around mental health – where I think it'd be more than fair to say that incorrect and inaccurate assumptions are made of them by 'outsiders' (people with little to no knowledge or experience of blogging in the mental health industry). I've found that setting a blogging goal is actually one of those because people without any connection to this industry believe it's just about saying "I want to reach another 100 readers in the next week." When, in fact, it can be much more intense and thought-provoking, and if you get that wrong – if you don't think your goals through thoroughly and effectively – then it would come as no surprise if it's more challenging for you to meet it.

As always, I'm incredibly aware and conscious that I can very easily and understandably come across as arrogant in giving advice, however I'd like to point out that SMART goals aren't my own invention at all! I actually only learnt about them in recent years when I began volunteering in the Communications and Marketing department at a local Hospice because SMART is very regularly used in designing strategies in that industry – particularly for social media and for pitching advertorial partnerships. However, I recognise that again, this is a more appropriate action for a blogger who is serious, dedicated, and determined to blog and to making their blog into something really special, important, and meaningful...

Specific

So, the first part of SMART is the 'S' standing for 'Specific' and this means ensuring that your goal is clear and concise.

Now, this might sound like a very obvious step or part to creating a goal because what is a goal without its title? But actually, it demands a fair bit of thought and consideration to determine a specific goal. You need to be able to feel that you have the phrasing of it correct and aligned with your actual intentions.

It's important that your goal is completely defined by yourself – that you choose the words used in it and that in doing so, you ensure it properly and effectively sums up exactly what you'd like to achieve. Without this clarity and concise nature, your goal can be vague and open to debate, discussion, uncertainty, and if it has this quality, it can very easily and understandably result in a degree of varied and contradictory thoughts as to whether or not you've even achieved or accomplished the goal!

Vague and general goals are actually very rarely met at all, because the absence of clarity and specific detail around them can really lend them to becoming forgettable and reduced in terms of priority. If you set a goal that is just labelled 'get more readers', then how can you really work towards that or deem yourself to have met it without requiring more information or a better understanding of just what you intended to accomplish when you set it? Having your goal be more specific and really narrowed down however, can massively help you in planning a strategy or a set of steps and stages to achieve it.

Measurable

Another essential component to creating a SMART goal for your blog or blogging career, is the 'M' which stands for 'Measurable.'

This aspect really refers to the importance of ensuring how you will keep track of your progress through the time and effort you put in to working towards your goal. Making your goal measurable in having some means of documenting where you are in terms of how much time it will take to achieve it or how much more effort you need to be putting in, can help you to stay more focused and productive.

Fortunately, with the advances in technology that we have today – particularly those that are especially useful to the communications and marketing industry (including those for blogs and social media platforms) – there are now so many tools, apps, and websites that can really aid you in measuring your progress with a SMART goal for your blog. Having this ability to discover some really incredible details about the majority of your readers – for instance, the time of the day that they are most active online - can really enhance your blog and your actual blogging. For example, you can use the knowledge of that time of the day when it is most popular for your average reader to be online, and publish a lot of your content at that time with the idea that there's a larger chance it will be viewed and/or responded to than if someone had to do a ton of scrolling back to find it.

Having an ability to measure your SMART goal is also useful in helping you to see the reality of your progress when it is recorded and factored into percentages etc. This can aid you in feeling more hopeful than if it were just down to you to decide whether you merely *felt* that you were making progress. If you're like me and you're not someone who can always blow their own trumpet confidently, it can be really difficult to fairly and objectively recognise your progress or achievements.

Achievable

The next letter in SMART: 'A,' stands for 'Achievable' and is centred around ensuring that your goal is realistic and is a reasonable aim that is surely practical and possible.

Towards the last few months of putting this Guide together, I was also trying to complete voluntary shifts as the Head of Marketing and Communications for a company, had to maintain my blog in continuing to produce content for I'm NOT Disordered, had appointments and meetings for various other commitments and projects, and started to create an entire Blogmas series (daily content from December 1st until Christmas Day)!

After a few months of this incredible frantic and stressful life, I recognised that I was no longer enjoying myself – with any of my commitments! – and that really upset me because I wanted to be able to say that the writing journey had been fun and exciting. So, I made the decision to end my contract with the voluntary role and found myself feeling more able to focus on putting this Guide together in time for its publication date – which seemed to be getting nearer incredibly quickly!

In all honesty though, I'm grateful for that difficult period because it has proven to have taught me a heck of a lot of really helpful lessons. They were particularly about how crucial and monumental prioritising can be and the importance of equally recognising both my strengths and the skills that I lack. It also taught me a lot about my capabilities and that has massively helped me to recognise if a goal I'm considering is actually realistic and manageable. Quitting my voluntary role, I've seen how much happier I am without that extra stress and pressure and that's been really important in teaching me that to recognise you can't do it all at once, isn't a weakness. It's not a failure or example of defeat. If anything, it's a sign of strength and bravery.

Relevant

The 'R' in 'SMART' refers to 'Relevance' and this concerns ensuring that your goal is aligned with longer-term values, commitments, and other objectives you may have or be working towards and aiming to achieve.

Having spent the best part of the last fourteen years feeling suicidal and making a handful of serious attempts to genuinely end my life, I actually still find thinking about long-term things in this sort of way, very strange and unfamiliar. Lacking experience in being able to confidently consider myself to have a future that is even just beyond the next week meant that when I started to take blogging seriously and began making big decisions for, I'm NOT Disordered, I was extremely anxious, nervous, hesitant, and reluctant. I think the most influential part of those feelings was the thought or belief that raced through my head around the conviction that if I were to think long-term and then – for whatever reason – couldn't reach the goal, I would feel like a complete failure and I worried how I would cope with that feeling.

Another difficulty for me to consider long-term commitments in connection with making the SMART goal relevant to them, was that despite the fact that I'm taking blogging more seriously, despite the fact that I do media interviews, despite the fact that I can see how many thousands of readers my blog is attracting per day; my blog's success, popularity, and the opportunities it affords me, have continued to surprise me. Massively and, even after ten years in the industry! It almost feels as though on a regular basis my dreams, hopes, and expectations are surpassed at a 'dream-come-true' level!

Timely

Finally, the 'T' in 'SMART' means for your goal to be 'Time-Based' in so far as having a realistic, but still ambitious deadline which should aid in prioritising tasks and increase levels of motivation.

In all honesty, it took quite a while before I had to learn about prioritising. When I first started blogging in 2013, because I was a psychiatric hospital inpatient my only real other commitments were the therapeutic timetable that scheduled our days during the week. Hours assigned to activities like reading group and self-harm awareness group and the very necessary and ultimately, compulsory Dialectical Behaviour Therapy (DBT) as groups and in weekly 1:1 session.

When I resumed my blogging after my discharge from the hospital, I found that I needed to start prioritising things because not only did I have I'm NOT Disordered, but I was also doing a distance learning course with a College and was finally able to start building my friendships back up with the people I had barely seen in the two and a half years I was in the hospital because it had been over 100 miles away from all of them.

In using this situation at the beginning of my learning curve in figuring out and establishing the importance of different tasks, meant that I started to recognise that having some sort of timeline or deadline for them could really aid in establishing how to determine my priorities properly, effectively, and in a more productive way. This (creating and determining or seeking deadlines) is something which has proven to be so helpful for me that it's now definitely a longstanding habit for me to encourage collaboration partners to decide on some sort of timeline for our work together.

I've also found having time frames for SMART goals useful where I've had multiple projects on the go at the same time, and there have been one or two that I've been enjoying working on the most. So, them having different deadlines has meant that I've been able to find the perfect balance between working on the tasks that really need to get finished first, and still be able to spend ample time and work on the bits that I might be enjoying more.

7 Helpful Tips to Achieve Your Goals

✓ Don't be afraid to say "no" to opportunities because of other commitments that are essential in achieving a goal

✓ Always prioritise according to date and time deadlines rather than by whatever you're most eager to work on

✓ Utilise all the stationary in the world(!) to properly plan, organise, and brainstorm your ideas and the process to make your goal a reality

✓ Engage in self-soothing activities that will put you into a better, more productive mood and wellbeing for working on your goals

✓ Know that it's ok to look to others who have had similar goals and be inspired by their methods for achieving these

✓ Aim to find a balance between working hard on your goals and doing some simple, fun, and enjoyable recreational activities and hobbies

✓ Don't be afraid to say that you need help from someone else to do some aspects of the goal – it's not a failure and it doesn't make you a failure

Are Achieving Your Goals Enough?

Aside from the best-friend with a blog, my largest inspiration in my blogging career is Victoria Magrath of inthefrow.com which might seem odd because she's really a fashion and beauty influencer (though she does occasionally feature some 'lifestyle' content that can lead to a chat around more personal aspects of her life). This has included sharing the difficult moments in her career so that whilst she mostly publishes positive and uplifting content, there's still an awareness of the imperfections in life and how both the negative and positive sides to doing this should be discussed or mentioned equally.

Whilst her focus on fashion and a beauty means that I can't exactly take much influence from, or in any remote ways replicate, her content; the influence I do take from following her social media and content creation is her work ethic. I completely recognise that so much goes on behind the scenes and having talked earlier in the Guide about how online influencers don't always publish the entirety of their life, I still often think that she feels the way that I do in one respect of blogging and that is around setting goals.

Like me, she seems to set her sights high and always strives to produce the best content she possibly can, whilst never stopping thinking about how it could still be improved. Some people may see this as unhealthy in that it makes it apparent that no matter which goal is achieved, it is never 100% satisfying because there's always the urge to create a new, bigger, and better one. I can actually, really understand the logic behind that because it might appear as though there's no time to actually stop and enjoy the achievement of a goal because the focus is on the next one.

This isn't true for me, though. I mean, anyone who knows me will say I love a good celebration or party, and I'm really mindful of illustrating an awareness and recognition of accomplishments. I think that this largely stems from the fact that whilst I have never really been one to blow my own trumpet, growing up; my achievements were always, hugely acknowledged and praised. I remember when I passed my GCSE exams when I was 16 and I went to see my Mum at work to tell her and she dragged me all around the building telling all her colleagues! Having just gone through the abuse (but at that point, no one knew about it yet), having so much warmth, kindness, and support was much needed and even more greatly appreciated.

My abuser was always telling me negative things about how I was useless, how I wouldn't amount to anything in life, that I deserved to fail my exams... I think that no matter who it is making those types of comments to you, if they say it enough times, it starts to grind into your mind and that can end up leaving an etched mark on the rest of your entire life. It's a bit of a bitter pill to swallow because it's almost as though you've been cut off at the knees before you even started the race. It almost left me wondering what the point was in doing anything that might possibly result in something even remotely positive because why would I believe I'd be capable of actually achieving it? Of reaching that point?

Those comments from my abuser over a six-month period are still being gradually – and very slowly – worn away by all the people I have in my life now who tell me the opposite. More importantly (in my opinion) and more monumental than that though, they're also being worn down by my own insight and recognition of all that I have achieved in my blogging career and in I'm NOT Disordered's journey. Earlier in the Guide I talked about how the most helpful tool I've found for providing me with some sense of confidence and assurance with this and in the thought that I'm doing a good job in the content I create, has been the gravity of the following my blog has. I 100% recognise though, that not every single person who has read my blog has enjoyed the content, but surely, I can't be doing too badly when you consider the reader count is on over 1.2 million now?!

I think that continually setting higher and higher goals one immediately after the other isn't necessarily a bad thing. Rather than it seeming as though it has meant that I don't stop and enjoy the benefits of one accomplishment, it's actually that I have stopped and enjoyed them and that those rewarding thoughts and feelings and experiences have ended up spurring me on to strive for bigger and better. Feeling proud of myself, being able to meet with someone I regard as important or special, receiving lovely comments from complete strangers, and being offered one-off opportunities, are all some of the many instances that, because I've struggled with my mental health for so long, I feel so eager to monopolise and enhance in whatever way possible.

The one downside to having so many ambitions and being so passionate and dedicated to improving my blog and the content I create that I will concede to, is the tiredness and drain this can put on your psychological strength and physical energy levels. It can sometimes feel as though you don't really have long to 'stop and smell the roses' before you're committing to another piece of work in collaboration with a huge organisation or are brainstorming a new series of content you feel you should do. However, in the face of all that is the recognition that I blog voluntarily. No one is forcing me to. I'm not doing it to earn a wage that I use to pay my bills. So, I recognise that really, a lot of this is within my control and that if I need to take a breather or if I think I'm drained or stressed because I'm trying to take on too much at once, then it's really up to me to do something about that.

In appreciating this though, I also acknowledge that the blogging industry is very much a competitive one. I have seen this grow more and more true rather than debatable throughout my journey with I'm NOT Disordered. Having started blogging with barely any well-known mental health blogs, I found a niche immediately and seeing how saturated the digital world is now with mental health themed content, I truly recognise how lucky I was for that. There are so many budding bloggers out there now who feel intimidated by the success of others, or who are dwarfed by more established, better connected, blogs/bloggers. I feel that it's almost an undebatable issue; you have to continue to better your content and your blog on a whole if you want to continue and progress (in whatever way you'd like or are aiming toward) in this industry.

Finally, I think that it's so important that in entering into the blogging industry you recognise – as best you can and as early on as you can – some of the hurdles you may be faced with. In doing so, you'll be provided with a level of preparation that can serve well in aiding you to not feel overwhelmed to the point where you feel the need to quit and close your blog.

Why?

Because we need more bloggers. The world needs more people who will be unafraid and undeterred in speaking the truth. People who will share their creativity with joy, excitement, and positivity. People who will be strong enough to share their story and who will bravely, passionately, and with great dedication, take on whatever may seem necessary in order to fulfil the prospect of helping so many others.

My universe will never be the same,

I'm glad you came

The Wanted – Glad You Came

Printed in Great Britain
by Amazon

34769893R00106